The Cherry Orchard

The
Cherry Orchard

Anton Chekhov

in a version by Pam Gems
from a literal translation by Tania Alexander

Edited by Brian Woolland

Series Editor: Judith Baxter

The publishers would like to thank Nicholas McGuinn and
Jane Ogborn for their help as consulting editors for the series.

Published by the Press Syndicate of the University of Cambridge
The Pitt Building, Trumpington Street, Cambridge CB2 1RP
40 West 20th Street, New York, NY 10011-4211, USA
10 Stamford Road, Oakleigh, Melbourne 3166, Australia

First published 1996

Printed in Great Britain by Scotprint, Musselburgh, Scotland

A catalogue record for this book is available from the British Library

ISBN 0 521 57670 9 paperback

Prepared for publication by Stenton Associates

Performing Rights: applications for performance in any medium and in
any language by professionals and amateurs throughout the world
should be addressed to Pam Gems's sole agent, Sebastian Born,
The Agency (London) Ltd, 24 Pottery Lane, London W11 4LZ.
Fax number: 0171 727 9037.

CONTENTS

✦

CAMBRIDGE LITERATURE

This edition of *The Cherry Orchard* is part of the Cambridge Literature series, and has been specially prepared for students in schools and colleges who are studying the play as part of their English course.

This study edition invites you to think about what happens when you read the play, and it suggests that you are not passively responding to words on the page which have only one agreed interpretation, but that you are actively exploring and making new sense of what you read and act out. Your 'reading' will partly stem from you as an individual, from your own experiences and point of view, and to this extent your interpretation will be distinctively your own. But your reading will also stem from the fact that you belong to a culture and a community, rooted in a particular time and place. So, your understanding may have much in common with that of others in your class or study group.

There is a parallel between the way you read this play and the way it was written. The Resource Notes at the end are devised to help you to investigate the complex nature of the writing and dramatisation process. The Resource Notes begin with the playwright's first ideas and sources of inspiration, move through to the stages of writing, publication and stage production, and end with the play's reception by the audience, reviewers, critics and students. So the general approach to study focuses on five key questions:

Who wrote *The Cherry Orchard* and why?

What type of play is it?

How was it produced?

How does it present its subject?

Who reads / watches *The Cherry Orchard*? How do they interpret it?

The text of *The Cherry Orchard* is presented complete and uninterrupted. Some words in the play have been glossed as they may be unfamiliar due to a particular cultural or linguistic significance.

The Resource Notes encourage you to take an active and imaginative approach to studying the play both in and out of the classroom. As well as providing you with information about many aspects of *The Cherry Orchard* they offer a wide choice of activities to work on individually, or in groups. Above all, they give you the chance to explore this poignant play in a variety of ways: as a reader, an actor, a researcher, a critic, and a writer.

Judith Baxter

INTRODUCTION

Anton Chekhov started writing *The Cherry Orchard* in early 1903. The play was first produced in January 1904. In July of that year Chekhov died of a heart attack at the age of forty-four. Since that first production, *The Cherry Orchard* has become increasingly popular. It has been translated into many languages and continues to be performed all over the world. Chekhov was a prolific writer, with numerous short stories and short plays to his credit, as well as four major plays, of which *The Cherry Orchard* was the last, and is probably the best known.

His early stories were light and humorous, as were most of his short plays. Known as vaudevilles, these plays feature comic characters (often exaggerated, sometimes even caricatures), and farcical situations. Many of them were reworkings of his own short stories. Although generally very light in tone, these short plays do contain elements in common with the more serious full-length plays. Much of the humour in the vaudevilles, for example, arises out of characters' mutual misunderstandings, and occasionally from their wilful refusal to accept the truth of a given situation. Although *The Cherry Orchard* is more complex (and the characterisation is deeper) than any of the vaudevilles, you will find that the characters' fixed attitudes and their unwillingness to accept the reality of the situation create both drama and humour.

When you go to the theatre or cinema or watch a television drama, the performances and production usually offer all sorts of clues in the first few minutes about what *sort* of drama you are going to be watching. As members of an audience to a comedy, for example, we are effectively told 'It's alright to laugh'. It's much more difficult to do this when you *read* a play for the first time because you are not able to see the details of performance, so it's useful to know something about the characters and their relationships before starting to read *The Cherry Orchard*.

BEFORE READING THE PLAY

Russian names: a guide to pronunciation

In general, all stressed 'a's are pronounced as in 'far' (written below as 'aa'); all stressed 'o's are pronounced as in 'more' (written below as 'aw'); unstressed 'a's and 'o's are slurred. The 'u's are pronounced as in 'crude' (written below as 'oo'). The stressed syllable in each name is indicated by *italics*.

Lyubov   Lyoo*bawf* or *Lyoo*ba And*ra*yevna Ran*yev*skaya
Anya   *Aa*nya
Varya   *Vaa*rya
Gayev   *Guy* (as in Guy Fawkes) yev
Yermolai Lopakhin   Yermo*lie* (as in 'lie' meaning deceive)
  Lo*paa*khin
Trofimov (Petya)   Tro*fee*mov (*Pyet* - ya; i.e. two syllables)
Semyonov-Pishchik   Sem*yaw*nov *Peesh*-cheek
Charlotta Ivanovna   Shar*lawt*a I*vaa*novna
Yepichodov   Yepi*khaw*dov
Dunyasha   Doon*yaash*a
Firs   (sounds like 'fierce')
Yasha   *Yaash*a

In different editions of *The Cherry Orchard*, you may well find that the characters' names are spelt slightly differently. This reflects the fact that the Russian and English alphabets and pronunciation are different. The spelling in this edition is intended to make the pronunciation easier.

Many English-speaking people find Russian names difficult to pronounce, and difficult to remember. The cast list gives the full Russian names, but when you first read the play you only need to remember the name by which the characters are known. Russian people traditionally have three names: their first name, their patronymic and a family name. The patronymic is their father's name plus either the suffix *-evna*, or *-ovna*, meaning 'daughter of', or *-evich*, meaning 'son of'. The family name is rarely used. Lyubov Andreyevna Ranyevskaya is known as Lyubov, her father's name was Andrey (Andrew in English) and her family name is Ranyevskaya – because she married someone of that name. Her brother is Leonid Andreyevich (son of Andrey) Gayev – Gayev being the family name that Lyubov would also have had before she married.

✦ Activities

The explanation above may sound complicated, but a simple practical exercise will make it easier to identify characters and recognise them when you come to read the play. As a group, allocate all the roles in the play between you, and organise yourselves as if you were preparing for a formal posed photograph of the characters of the play on the estate. You do not need to 'play' the roles, simply to position yourselves in relation to each other and say aloud the name of the character you represent.

- **Lyubov** stands with **Gayev** – sister and brother;
- Close to Lyubov is her daughter, **Anya**, and nearby **Varya**, her adopted daughter;
- Anya is attended by **Charlotta** (the governess who has travelled with Lyubov and Anya to Paris). Perhaps watching Anya from a little distance is **Petya Trofimov**, the student who is awaiting their return;
- **Semyonov-Pishchik**, the neighbouring landowner, might also be trying to get in on the photograph; but he's not actually part of the family.
- Then there are the four servants: **Dunyasha**, the young chambermaid, **Yepichodov**, the estate clerk, **Yasha**, the young footman who went to Paris with Lyubov, and **Firs**, the old man who has worked for the family all his life. These four have relationships between themselves, and with the family. But they will be a little way away from the main family group.

- Finally there is **Lopakhin**, the businessman. Perhaps he has arrived late for the photograph; but is keen to speak to Lyubov.

When you have made the group, each speak aloud the following lines from various points in the play. They will, again, help you to identify the characters, and differentiate between them when you read the play for yourself.

LYUBOV	Oh my lovely, innocent childhood. ... Oh, my dear orchard.
ANYA	A whole new world will open up for us.
VARYA	I can't bear the thought of having nothing to do. ... All this joking. I take it seriously.
GAYEV	What I've been through. ... How can I refrain from expressing my emotions.
LOPAKHIN	Done well for meself. Still a peasant though.
TROFIMOV	The perpetual student it seems. ... We must go forward, friends.
PISHCHIK	Money, money – I never seem to think of anything else. ... Lend me two hundred.
CHARLOTTA	I am quite alone. ... One more trick.
FIRS	I've lived a long time. ... In the old days you knew where you were.
YEPICHODOV	Every day something goes wrong.
DUNYASHA	I feel all faint. My hands are trembling.
YASHA	I'm not very keen on girls who make fools of themselves. ... It's so boring; I'm sure Madame understands.

When you have read the play you may want to return to this exercise, organising the characters in other ways; and considering whether there are other lines from the play which are particularly characteristic. There are further exercises on characterisation in the Resource Notes (on pages 110 to 114).

READING THE PLAY

In most dramas (whether they are on film, television or for the theatre) there is a single character at the centre of the action. The audience sees most of the events of the play (or film) through the experiences of this central character. One of the great pleasures of *The Cherry Orchard* is the richness and variety of its characterisation, and the number of different relationships that Chekhov depicts. This richness can make reading *The Cherry Orchard* more difficult than reading a play in which there are only a few characters who are fully drawn.

✦ *Activity*

As you read *The Cherry Orchard*:

a Try to identify the central character. Whose story is it?

b Note the various relationships. You could do this in note form, or use diagrams with captions to show visually the connections between the different characters.

c The play is set on an old estate in rural Russia. Chekhov doesn't say exactly where it is, although he does give various clues, through reference to other places. As you read the play, make a note of those occasions when characters refer to places away from the estate. See whether you can identify these on a map of Europe.

d Note what you expect of the play and of the characters – particularly at the end of each of the first three acts, and at the moment just before the family arrive (on page 17).

e Although the play contains much that is serious, Chekhov stated many times that he intended it as a comedy. He said, for example, in a letter to his wife in 1901: 'The next play that I write will definitely be a very funny one ...' In spite of this there have been many productions of the play (including the first in 1904) which have ignored the play's comic elements. As you read the play, note down those stage directions which suggest comic business, slapstick or visual humour of any kind; and also any examples of dialogue where there are misunderstandings between characters which might make an audience laugh. (See also the Resource Notes on 'Comedy in *The Cherry Orchard*', on pages 91–93).

Acknowledgements

This version of *The Cherry Orchard* is by Pam Gems. Her work as a playwright includes *Camille*, *Piaf*, *The Blue Angel*, and (most recently) *Stanley* (premiered at the Royal National Theatre, London, in 1996). Her highly acclaimed versions of Chekhov's *Uncle Vanya* and *The Seagull* were also produced at the Royal National Theatre.

The photograph on page 104 shows Act 2 of *The Cherry Orchard*, directed by Giorgio Strehler, Piccolo Teatro di Milano, 1974: l. to r.: Piero Sammataro as Trofimov, Monica Guerritone as Anya, Valentina Cortese as Lyubov, Franco Graciozi as Lopakhin, Giulia Lazzarini as Varya and Gianni Santuccio as Gayev.
Photograph by Ciminaghi.

Brian Woolland, the editor, is a lecturer in drama at Reading University and a freelance playwright, whose work has been performed in several European countries.

THE CAST

Note that in the following cast list the words which appear in bold type are the names by which the characters are identified in the dialogue.

Lyubov Andreyevna Ranyevskaya (Lyuba):
　　　a land-owning widow
Anya (Anushka):
　　　her daughter, aged 17
Varya (Varvara Mihailovna):
　　　her adopted daughter, aged 24
Leonid Andreyevich **Gayev** (Lenya):
　　　Lyubov's brother
Yermolai Alexeyevich **Lopakhin**:
　　　a businessman
Pyotr Borisovich **Trofimov** (Petya):
　　　a student
Boris Borisovich Semyonov-**Pishchik**:
　　　a neighbouring landowner
Charlotta Ivanovna:
　　　the governess
Semyon Panteleyevich **Yepichodov**:
　　　the estate clerk
Dunyasha (Avdotya Fyodorovna):
　　　the maid
Firs Nicolayevich:
　　　the old footman, aged 87
Yasha:
　　　the young footman
A Man:
　　　a drunken passer-by
The Station-master
Guests at a ball
Servants

Act One

[*Early dawn. The old nursery,* ° *with several doors, one of them to* ANYA's *bedroom. Outside there is frost on the cherry orchard.*]

LOPAKHIN It's here, is it? Thank God. What's the time?

DUNYASHA Nearly two, light already. [*She blows out the candle.*]

LOPAKHIN Train must have been two hours late. [*He yawns and stretches.*] Ugh. … I'm a fool. Idiot – I come here specially to go and meet them and what do I do? I fall asleep … sitting up! I was going to the station, why didn't you wake me?

DUNYASHA I thought you'd gone. [*She listens.*] Ssh, I think I can hear them.

  [*LOPAKHIN listens.*]

LOPAKHIN No-o. There'll be all the luggage … one thing and another …

  [*Pause.*]

  Lyubov Andreyevna! Five years! It's going to be funny seeing her again, I wonder if she's changed. Fine woman – well, she was. Straightforward. Very easy to talk to. I remember once, when I was a lad … it was when we had the shop, I must have been about fifteen. My nose was bleeding, my father'd hit me in the face … drunk … anyway, we'd come up here for something or other. Very young she was then. Very … slender. She brought me right in here, right into the nursery as it then was, to the washstand, to rinse the blood off. "Don't cry, little peasant" she said "you'll be all right for your wedding day!" [*Pause.*] Little peasant. True. Son of a peasant. And here I stand, in a white weskit

15

and yellow boots like a pig in a pastry shop. Done well for meself. Still a peasant though, eh? [*Picks up the book that has fallen from his lap, flicks the pages.*] See this? Don't understand a word of it – sent me to sleep! [*Pause.*]

DUNYASHA The dogs have been awake all night … they know she's coming! They know!

LOPAKHIN What's up with you?

DUNYASHA I feel all faint … my hands are trembling!

LOPAKHIN Too many fancy ideas, that's your trouble. Done up like a lady – your hair all – you're not a lady, what's the matter with you?

[*YEPICHODOV enters, carrying a bunch of flowers. His boots squeak. He drops the flowers.*]

YEPICHODOV The gardener sent these, he says they're for the dining room. [*He scrambles, picking up the flowers, giving them to DUNYASHA, who goes off with them.*]

LOPAKHIN And bring me a drink!

DUNYASHA Yes sir! [*As she goes.*]

YEPICHODOV The cherry trees covered in blossom and three degrees of frost this morning! [*Sighs.*] I don't think much of our climate, Yermolai Alexeyevich. You can't say it helps. What's more – what's more, the day before yesterday I bought myself a new pair of boots which, if you don't mind my saying, squeak so badly – I mean, what are you supposed to do? What sort of grease d'you think?

LOPAKHIN Look shut up, will you?

YEPICHODOV There's always something. Every day – every day something goes wrong. I mean, I'm not complaining about it, I don't let it get me down, I have a laugh about it … haha. [*DUNYASHA enters with a drink for LOPAKHIN.*] Yes, well, I'll … [*He knocks over a chair at the sight of her.*] See? I mean you have

to – it's more than … it's not a coincidence, you know
… [*He goes.*]

DUNYASHA Still, he has asked me to marry him, Yermolai
Alexeyevich.

LOPAKHIN Oho!

DUNYASHA I don't know what to think. He's a nice, quiet
man, only when he says anything you can't understand
a word of it. It all sounds lovely – you know,
cultivated – only none of it makes sense. I mean I don't
dislike him, and he's mad with passionate love for me
of course. It's just that … we-ell … he's unlucky. There
isn't a day when something doesn't … you know what
they call him – 'One Foot in the Cowpat'!°

LOPAKHIN Listen, is that them?

DUNYASHA Ooh they're here, what's the matter with me,
I've gone cold all over!

LOPAKHIN Yes, it's them. Come on. I wonder if she'll
recognise me, it's five years.…

DUNYASHA Oh I feel faint, I feel faint!

[*They go quickly. Sounds of arrival. FIRS enters. He
wears old-fashioned livery, leans on a stick and mutters
to himself. The sound of voices.*]

ANYA Let's go this way.

[*LYUBOV ANDREYEVNA enters, followed by ANYA
and CHARLOTTA IVANOVNA, who has a dog on a
lead. All are dressed for travelling. VARYA wears a coat
and a headscarf. They are followed by GAYEV,
SEMYONOV-PISHCHIK, LOPAKHIN, DUNYASHA,
who carries a bundle and an umbrella, and a servant with
luggage.*]

ANYA Mama … remember?

LYUBOV [*With emotion.*] The nursery!

VARYA Ugh, it's cold, my hands are numb. [*To LYUBOV
ANDREYEVNA.*] We've left your rooms, Mama dear
… the lavender and the white, just as they were.…

LYUBOV The nursery! My dear, darling room … [*She cries.*] I used to sleep here when I was little. I feel a child again. [*She kisses her brother, then VARYA, then her brother again.*] And Varya looks just the same – my same little nun! Dunyasha … it's Dunyasha! [*She kisses DUNYASHA.*]

GAYEV Two hours late. How is it possible for a train to be two hours late? What a country.

CHARLOTTA [*To SEMYONOV-PISHCHIK, pointing to her dog.*] He eats nuts!

PISHCHIK Unbelievable!

[*LYUBOV ANDREYEVNA, GAYEV, LOPAKHIN, CHARLOTTA and SEMYONOV-PISHCHIK go. Only ANYA and DUNYASHA are left.*]

DUNYASHA We've been waiting and waiting for you! [*She takes off ANYA's hat and coat.*]

ANYA I couldn't sleep on the train, I haven't slept for four whole nights – oh, I'm so frozen!

DUNYASHA You went away in the snow and the cold, and now look! Oh you lovely, lovely, lovely … ooh, you're back…. [*Laughing and kissing ANYA.*] I've been waiting and waiting – there's something to tell you, I can't keep it in another minute, I'm going to burst! …

ANYA What is it this time?

DUNYASHA It's Yepichodov …, the clerk! He proposed! Just after Holy Week!

ANYA Here we go again … [*She arranges her hair.*] I've lost every single hairpin.

DUNYASHA I don't know what to do, he's madly in love with me!

ANYA [*Looks lovingly into her bedroom.*] My own room. My own windows. I'm home again. I feel as though I'd never been away. Tomorrow I'll get up and run straight into the garden…. Oh, I must sleep, I couldn't on the journey, I was so worried.

Dunyasha Trofimov's here!

Anya Petya?

Dunyasha He's staying in the bathhouse, he says he
    doesn't want to be in the way. I was going to wake
    him up but Varya said "Oh don't wake *him* up!"
        [*VARYA enters, keys at her waist.*]

Varya Quick, Dunyasha, make some coffee, Mama's
    asking for coffee.

Dunyasha I won't be long. [*She goes.*]

Varya Thank God … you're back at last. [*She embraces
    ANYA.*] My own precious beauty … you're home.

Anya What a time!

Varya I can imagine.

Anya Remember how cold it was in Holy Week? – I
    thought I'd die on that train. And stupid Charlotta
    doing her stupid conjuring tricks all the way…. She
    never stops talking, why on earth did you make me
    take her?

Varya Because you're seventeen, darling. You can't travel
    without a chaperone.

Anya When we got there it was snowing. In Paris! My
    French is useless, Mama's on the fifth floor, when I
    arrive she's surrounded by Frenchmen … people,
    women I don't know. There's an old priest in the
    corner with his book – the whole place is reeking with
    cigarette smoke, oh, and everything so uncomfortable!
    I suddenly felt so sorry for Mama, I just put my hands
    on her face and held her, I just couldn't let her go. And
    afterwards she hugged and hugged and hugged me,
    and cried.

Varya Don't. I can't bear it.

Anya She's already sold the villa in Menton.° There's
    nothing left. I haven't a kopek° … there was hardly
    enough to get us back. Mama doesn't seem to
    understand. We sit down at the station restaurant …

she orders the most expensive thing on the menu, and then tips the waiters a rouble° each. Charlotta's just as bad, and Yasha's been eating his way through full course dinners – you know he's the valet now?

VARYA Yes, I've seen him, the rogue.

ANYA Tell me, how is everything? Was the interest paid?

VARYA With what?

ANYA Oh God, oh God …

VARYA The estate's up for sale. August.

ANYA No!

LOPAKHIN [*Looks in the door and bleats like a sheep to indicate their chatter.*] Meh-eh-eh-eh! [*He goes.*]

VARYA [*Shakes her fist.*] I'll give him such a –

ANYA [*Embraces VARYA.*] Has he proposed yet? [*VARYA shakes her head.*] Look, why not have it out? You know he loves you, what are you waiting for?

VARYA I don't think anything will come of it. He never takes the slightest notice of me – he's busy all the time! All it does is make me miserable, listening to everyone talking about it…. "I hear you're getting married, when's the big day?" – there's nothing in it, it's all wishwash. [*Change of tone.*] You've got a new brooch. Is it a bee?

ANYA [*Sad for VARYA.*] Mama bought it for me. [*But her mood changes as she goes into her room and she talks happily, like a child.*] You'll never guess! … in Paris I went up in a balloon!

VARYA Oh my love, my precious beauty … you're home!
   [*DUNYASHA returns and prepares the coffee. VARYA stands by the door to ANYA's room.*]
You know dearest, when I'm here working about the house you know what's in my mind? Just over and over … if only you could marry some nice fine man with lots and lots of money. I wouldn't have to worry then. I could just go away. I'd be off on my own, first

20

to a retreat … then Kiev° … Moscow … I'd walk to all the holy places … walk and walk and walk – oh, what bliss!

Anya [*Calls.*] I can hear the birds singing in the orchard! What time is it?

Varya It's after two and you should be in bed, my love.
[*She goes into ANYA's room. YASHA enters with a rug and a small case.*]

Yasha All right to go through here?

Dunyasha Yasha! I wouldn't have recognised you!

Yasha Hmmm – what's your name?

Dunyasha It's me! Dunyasha! You remember! Fyodor Kosoyedov's daughter. I was only this high when you left!

Yasha Mmm. Quite a little pumpkin. [*He looks round swiftly then embraces her. She yells and drops a saucer. YASHA leaves.*]

Varya [*In the doorway.*] What's going on?

Dunyasha [*Upset.*] I've broken a saucer.

Varya Oh have you? Never mind, it'll bring us luck.

Anya [*Enters.*] We ought to warn Mama that Petya's here.

Varya They were told not to wake him.

Anya Six years. I can't believe it. Losing Papa and then my darling little brother – oh Grisha … all in a month! How could she bear it? That dear, sweet little boy, drowned! Seven years old! No wonder she went away, I want to say – Mama, I understand – I want her to know …
[*Pause.*]
Yes. It'll remind her, seeing Petya … seeing his tutor.
[*FIRS enters in a jacket and a white waistcoat.*]

Firs [*Fusses over coffee pot.*] The mistress wants it in here…. [*Puts on his white gloves.*] Is it ready? [*To DUNYASHA, stern.*] You – where's the cream?

Dunyasha Ooh Lord! [*She dashes off.*]

FIRS Good-for-nothing! [*Mutters over pot.*] Been to Paris have they … he used to go there … Master … horses it was then … trains! … [*He laughs to himself.*]

VARYA Firs, what are you laughing at?

FIRS She's just bringing it. [*Joyfully.*] No more waiting … she's home! I've hung on … don't care if I die now. [*He wipes his eyes with joy.*]

> [*Enter LYUBOV ANDREYEVNA, GAYEV, PISHCHIK, who wears a long Russian coat of fine cloth, tight at the waist, with loose Turkish trousers, and LOPAKHIN. GAYEV is making movements with his hands and body as if playing billiards.*◦]

LYUBOV [*Laughing.*] How does it go? Let me try and remember … the yellow into the corner … then I double into the middle!

GAYEV Screw shot into the corner – ah, here we are! There was a time when we slept in here, brother and sister together. And now I'm fifty-one. Hard to believe.

LOPAKHIN Yes, time flies.

GAYEV Who?

LOPAKHIN I was saying, time flies.

GAYEV Strong smell of patchouli◦ in here.

ANYA I'm going to bed. Goodnight, Mama. [*She kisses her mother.*]

LYUBOV My precious child. [*She kisses ANYA's hands.*] Are you happy to be home? I still can't believe I'm here.

ANYA Goodnight, Uncle.

> [*GAYEV kisses her hands and face.*]

GAYEV [*Kissing her fondly.*] God bless you, dearest … oh, how like your mother you are … Lyuba, she looks just as you did at her age. [*ANYA shakes hands with PISHCHIK and LOPAKHIN and goes.*]

LYUBOV She's so tired.

PISHCHIK Long way, to be sure.

Varya [*To LOPAKHIN and PISHCHIK.*] Well,
gentlemen … it's after two o'clock. Time to go.

Lyubov [*Laughs.*] Oh, Varya, you haven't changed! [*She
hugs VARYA.*] Let me drink my coffee and we'll all go
to bed. [*FIRS puts a cushion under her feet.*] Thank
you, my dear. I'm used to coffee now, I drink it all the
time. Thank you, dear old friend. [*She embraces FIRS
and kisses him.*]

Varya I'd better see if everything's been brought in. [*She
goes.*]

Lyubov Am I really back? Is it really me sitting here? I feel
like jumping and waving my arms about. Suppose it's
all a dream? Oh God, how I love this country! Such
feelings! On the train I was so full of tears I couldn't
even see out of the window! Well, I must drink up my
coffee – thank you, Firs, thank you, you dear old man
… praise the Lord you're still with us.

Firs The day before yesterday.

Gayev [*To LYUBOV ANDREYEVNA.*] Very deaf.

Lopakhin [*Jumps up.*] I must leave. There's a train for
Kharkov° at four. What a nuisance. I wanted a good
look at you, and a talk. You're as lovely as ever.

Pishchik [*Breathing heavily.*] Lovelier … lovelier … all
this Paris finery, enough to make a man lose his reins,
stirrups and all!

Lopakhin We know what your brother, we know what
Leonid Andreyevich thinks of me … just a cunning
peasant out for what he can get … well, he can think
what he likes. So long as you believe in me. Just so
long as you go on looking at me with those wonderful,
trusting eyes, the same as ever. I mean, merciful God,
when you think of it, my father was a serf! Your father
and grandfather owned him! But you're not the same.
You're different. With you I forget all of it. What I

remember is what you did for me, I don't forget that. You're more to me than my own flesh and blood.

LYUBOV I can't sit still.... I just can't sit still! [*She walks about, agitated.*] All this happiness ... it's just too much ... I shall never survive!

[*She roams about the room, touching things.*] Laugh at me if you want, I don't mind ... I just can't help myself, I know I'm a fool – oh, my own dear bookcase! [*She kisses the bookcase.*] And my little table!

GAYEV You heard about Nyanya?

LYUBOV I had a letter, yes. God rest her soul. [*She sits, drinks her coffee.*]

GAYEV Anastasy died too. And cross-eyed Petruchka – well, left us to go and work with the police. [*He takes a box of fruit drops from his pocket, takes one out and sucks it.*]

PISHCHIK My daughter – Dashenka – wishes to be remembered to you.

LOPAKHIN I wish I had good news for you. [*Looks at his watch.*] Look, I must go but this won't take a minute, I can say it in a few words. As it stands, the cherry orchard is up for sale on August the twenty-second to clear your debts. Well – stop worrying. You can sleep in peace, dear lady – could you listen, please? You're not more than twenty versts° from town and the railway's just there. All you have to do – divide up the orchard and the land down by the river into plots ... build dachas,° little cottages for the summer, rent them out and you'll have an income of twenty thousand roubles a year ... twenty at least!

GAYEV What? Don't be ridiculous!

LYUBOV Yermolai Alexeyevich, I'm sorry – what did you say?

24

Lopakhin You can charge each tenant twenty-five roubles a year per hectare per plot ... easily. If you advertise right away I guarantee by the autumn you won't have a single plot left ... they'll all be taken ... in a word – congratulations! You're saved! It's a wonderful site – beautiful river, deep water for bathing, all it needs is putting in order. You want to pull down all the old buildings, this place will have to go of course, not worth anything now ... cut down the cherry orchard –

Lyubov What? What did you say?

Lopakhin The cherry orchard. Cut it down.

Lyubov Cut it down? The cherry orchard? Are you serious? Don't you understand? This cherry orchard is the most remarkable ... if there is one interesting feature in this whole province, why then it's our cherry orchard!

Lopakhin The only thing that's remarkable about this cherry orchard is its size. It only produces a crop every other year, then there are so many nobody wants them.

Gayev This cherry orchard is mentioned in the Encyclopaedia!

Lopakhin [*Looks at his watch.*] Which doesn't alter the fact that if you don't come to an agreement pretty quickly both the orchard and the estate are going to be sold over your heads. Make up your minds! Take my word for it, there's no other way, I swear to you – none at all. None.

Firs We used to dry them in the sun in the old days. Then there was all the jam-making, and some we'd preserve in sugar, and some in jars and bottles, and some they used to soak in –

Gayev That's enough, Firs.

Firs We'd even send cartloads to Moscow ... Kharkov – they brought good money! Oh, they were sweet, those dried cherries, they had a scent on them … juicy and soft … they knew how to do it then … the old way ….

LYUBOV Who knows now?

FIRS Aye. Nobody. All gone and forgotten.

PISHCHIK [*To LYUBOV ANDREYEVNA.*] How did you get on in Paris? Did you eat frogs?

LYUBOV I ate crocodile!

PISHCHIK Unbelievable!

LOPAKHIN You must try to understand. Things have changed. It used to be just the gentry and the peasants. But now there's a new sort of visitor … people who want to come here in the summer. All the towns now are surrounded by dachas, even the smallest ones. In the next twenty years it's going to increase twenty fold. At first they just want to build themselves a verandah and sit and drink tea, but give them time. You'll see … soon they'll start making gardens for themselves and cultivating the ground. Your cherry orchard will be full of people – life – prosperity … everybody rich and happy …

GAYEV Ridiculous! Absolute nonsense!

[*VARYA and YASHA enter.*]

VARYA Mother darling, there are two telegrams for you. [*She selects a key and noisily unlocks an old bookcase.*] Ah, here they are.

LYUBOV [*Looks at the telegrams.*] From Paris. No. [*She tears them up.*] That's all over.

GAYEV Lyuba, do you realise how old it is? The bookcase! I pulled out the bottom drawer last week and there was the date, burned in the wood. This bookcase was made exactly a hundred years ago … think of that! A centenarian – we should celebrate! An inanimate object I grant you but – whichever way you look at it … a … a bookcase!

PISHCHIK A hundred years! Unbelievable!

GAYEV Yes ... quite a thing, eh? [*He feels the bookcase.*]
Dear, beloved, respected bookcase ... I salute you! I
salute your very existence which for over a hundred
years has served the ideals of virtue and justice. You
have stood there, your voice calling out to us ...
silently ... exhorting us to work ... inspiring
generation after generation of this family with courage
... with faith ... with belief in a better future. You,
bookcase, have instilled and fostered in us all our
ideals ... our standards ... of virtue ... of nobility ...
and social consciousness.

   [*Pause.*]

LOPAKHIN Yes ....

LYUBOV Still the same old Lenya.

GAYEV [*A little confused.*] Into the corner off the right ...
screw shot into the middle ...

LOPAKHIN [*Looks at his watch.*] Time to go.

YASHA [*To LYUBOV ANDREYEVNA.*] Do you want to
take your pills now? [*He hands her a bottle of pills.*]

PISHCHIK Pills ... pills? What do you want those for? You
don't want pills, dear lady – what good do pills do?
On the other hand – [*He grabs the bottle, swallows all
the pills.*] – what harm? There you are ... so much for
pills!

LYUBOV My dear, you're mad ... you'll be ill!

PISHCHIK Down in one, that's the way to do it!

LOPAKHIN He likes his stomach!

   [*They all laugh.*]

FIRS [*Mutters.*] ... ate half a bucket of cucumbers during
Lent.

LYUBOV What is he saying?

VARYA He does it all the time now ... we don't take any
notice.

YASHA He's past it!

27

[*CHARLOTTA IVANOVNA crosses the stage wearing a white dress tightly laced, a lorgnette° hanging on her belt. She is very thin.*]

LOPAKHIN Charlotta Ivanovna ... beg pardon – haven't had a chance to – [*He tries to kiss her hand.*]

CHARLOTTA [*Drawing her hand away.*] Hey, hey, hey!

LOPAKHIN Why not?

CHARLOTTA First the hand ... then the elbow ... then the shoulder – where will it end?

LOPAKHIN Out of luck, dammit! [*Laughter.*] Let's have a trick, Charlotta Ivanovna!

LYUBOV Yes, why not?

CHARLOTTA No. I wish to sleep. [*Goes.*]

LOPAKHIN [*Kisses LYUBOV ANDREYEVNA's hand.*] We'll meet again in three weeks – goodbye for now. [*To GAYEV.*] Goodbye. [*He embraces PISHCHIK.*] Goodbye. [*He shakes hands with VARYA, then FIRS and YASHA.*] I don't want to go. [*To LYUBOV ANDREYEVNA.*] If you make up your mind about the dachas, let me know. I can raise fifty thousand, no trouble, start the whole thing off. You will think about it?

VARYA Are you going or not?

LOPAKHIN I'm going, I'm going! [*Goes.*]

GAYEV The man's a boor. Oh. Pardon [*With a French accent.*] ... I forgot. Varya's going to marry him. He's the precious fiancé, isn't he?

VARYA Uncle, please.

LYUBOV I shall be very happy, Varya. He's a good man.

PISHCHIK No use denying it ... very good fellow – Dashenka says so. Mind you, she says he's a ... well, she says different things. [*He drops off, snores, wakes himself up.*] Oh by the way ... could I have the loan of two hundred and forty roubles, dear lady? The interest on my mortgage is due –

Varya We haven't got it!

Lyubov I really haven't anything at all.

Pishchik Never mind. Something will turn up. [*He laughs.*] I never lose hope. I remember one time, I thought I was finished ... lo and behold, they make up their minds to run the railway through my land, bless me, they pay me for it! Something will turn up, if not today, tomorrow ... Dashenka could win two hundred thousand on the lottery – she's got a ticket!

Lyubov There, the coffee's finished. We can all go to bed.

Firs [*Brushing GAYEV down.*] Tch, he's done it again – the wrong trousers! What are we to do with you?

Varya [*Softly.*] Anya's asleep. [*She opens the window quietly.*] The sun's up already. You can feel the warmth. Mama ... the trees ... aren't they marvellous! Oh, the air! And the starlings are singing!

Gayev [*Opens the other window.*] Blossom – all white. You haven't forgotten, Lyuba? The long straight avenue like a band stretched across the orchard and how it shines in the moonlight? Do you remember? You haven't forgotten?

Lyubov [*Looks through the window at the orchard.*] Oh my lovely innocent childhood! Sleeping here in the nursery, looking out into the orchard, ... every morning waking up to happiness. And here it is ... the same, just the same as it was, nothing's changed. [*She laughs with delight.*] All white ... oh my dear orchard! Stormy autumn, wicked cold winter and here you are, young and fresh and full of happiness again, ... all the darkness over, the angels haven't forsaken you. Oh, if only I could be rid of it ... the weight ... here.... [*She clasps her hands over her heart.*] Just forget ... if only you could! ...

Gayev Yes. The orchard. And now it will be sold to pay our debts.

LYUBOV Look, there's Mother! Walking towards us in a white dress! [*She laughs happily.*] There – over there!

GAYEV Where?

VARYA Lord save you, Mama!

LYUBOV I just imagined it. Look, over there, by the path to the summer house … the little tree bending over … it looks like a woman …

[*TROFIMOV enters in a faded student uniform and wearing glasses.*]

Beautiful, wonderful orchard … and the blossom so white against the blue …

TROFIMOV Lyubov Andreyevna …

[*She turns and sees him.*]

I won't stay. I just want to pay my respects. [*He kisses her hand with emotion.*] I was told to wait till morning, but I couldn't.

[*She looks at him, puzzled.*]

VARYA [*Gently.*] It's Pyotr Trofimov.

TROFIMOV Pyotr Trofimov … Petya … your son's tutor. Have I changed so much?

[*LYUBOV ANDREYEVNA embraces him and weeps.*]

GAYEV Come Lyuba, it's all right … it's all right.

VARYA [*Wiping her eyes.*] Petya, why didn't you wait, I asked you to wait until tomorrow.

LYUBOV My Grisha … my boy … my little boy … Grisha … my son …

VARYA There's nothing we can do, Mama. It was God's will.

TROFIMOV [*Crying.*] There … oh please … don't …

LYUBOV My little boy was drowned. Why? Why, my friend? Oh what am I doing? … Anya's asleep and I'm making a noise, I'm disturbing her. But Petya, you've lost your – you look so much older …

TROFIMOV The flea-bitten gent … that's what an old peasant woman on the train called me.

LYUBOV You were such a young boy! A nice young student. Your hair's not thick any more … you wear glasses … surely you're not still studying?

TROFIMOV Yes, the perpetual student,° it seems.

LYUBOV Off to bed now. [*She kisses her brother.*] You're getting old too, Lenya. [*She kisses VARYA.*]

PISHCHIK [*Following her off.*] Off to bed are we? Right – ooh ah ah ah … ooh, my gout! I'll stay here the night. Tomorrow morning, Lyubov Andreyevna, dearest heart, the loan of two hundred and forty, if you would … it's this mortgage –

GAYEV Always the same. Never gives up.

PISHCHIK Just a matter of the two hundred and forty … it's to keep up the interest, d'you see?

LYUBOV But my dear I've no money at all!

PISHCHIK Just a trifling sum … pay you back, of course …

LYUBOV Very well … yes … all right. Leonid will see to it … give it to him, Lenya.

GAYEV Naturally, of course … anything he wants, help yourself. Nothing doing.

LYUBOV But what can we do, he needs it! Give it to him. You know he'll pay us back.

[*She goes, with TROFIMOV, FIRS and SEMYONOV-PISHCHIK.*]

GAYEV My dear sister – still throwing her money away. [*To YASHA.*] You – clear out … you smell of the hen house.

YASHA [*Grins.*] You haven't changed, Leonid Andreyevich.

GAYEV [*As a snub.*] Who? [*To VARYA.*] What's he say?

VARYA [*To YASHA.*] Your mother's here, I wish you'd go and see her, she's been sitting in the servants' hall for the last two days.

YASHA Oh never mind her!

VARYA You should be ashamed of yourself.

YASHA What do I want to see her for, why didn't she wait till tomorrow? [*He goes.*]

VARYA Dear Mama. Always the same, she'd give everything away.

GAYEV Yes.

[*Pause.*]

When you're offered a thousand remedies you can be sure the disease is incurable. I've been wracking my brains! Thought of this ... thought of that ... hundreds of ideas ... nothing. If we could only inherit – marry Anya off to a rich man! Perhaps we could go to Yaroslavl,° try our luck with the Countess – very rich woman, my old aunt.

VARYA [*Sniffling.*] If only God would put out a hand to us!

GAYEV Don't blubber. No, the old Countess is in funds – she could spare us a rouble or two. Trouble is, she's never been the same since my sister's wedding. Not quite the thing, d'you see, marrying a lawyer. Bit of a comedown.

[*ANYA appears in the doorway.*]

And of course you couldn't say she's a model of virtue, my sister. Splendid woman ... very kind ... good-hearted – I love her very much. But whichever way you look at it ... I mean, even granted the circumstances, you must admit the life she leads – well, hardly moral, is it? You've only got to look at her ... the way she moves ...

VARYA [*Whispers.*] Sssh, Anya's there!

GAYEV Who? What? Oh. Funny, I've got something in my right eye. Well, as I was saying ... when I was down at the courts on Thursday –

VARYA Anya, why aren't you asleep?

ANYA I can't ... I've tried.

GAYEV [*Kissing her face and hands.*] My little one … dear child, you're not my niece you're an angel. You're everything to me, believe me, oh believe –

ANYA Uncle I do! Dear, darling Uncle, we all love and respect you but please, please, please be quiet! How can you say these things about Mother – your own sister!

GAYEV I know … I know! [*He covers his face with his hands.*] It's dreadful, God forgive me! And that speech I made to the bookcase … nonsense! I knew as soon as I stopped!

VARYA It's true, Uncle. If only you'd keep quiet – you shouldn't talk so much.

ANYA You'd feel better if you didn't say such things.

GAYEV I know. I promise. Silence. [*He kisses their hands.*] Just one more thing – it is business! I was down at the district court last Thursday, and well, there was quite a gathering and we were talking … about this and that, and do you know, it rather looks as though we might be able to raise a loan, against promissory notes, to pay off the bank interest.

VARYA Oh Lord, please help us!

GAYEV I'll go in again on Tuesday and have another talk about it.… [*To VARYA.*] Stop snivelling. [*To ANYA.*] Your Mother can talk to Lopakhin, he won't refuse her, and as soon as you've had a rest we'll send you to Yaroslavl to charm the old Aunt. Three-pronged attack, that's the way to do it. We'll find the money, pay the interest, I'm convinced of it. … [*Pops a fruit drop in his mouth.*] I'll swear on – on my honour, or whatever you want … this estate shall not be sold! [*Getting excited.*] I'll swear on my own happiness … look here's my hand! Call me a wretch and a lying rogue if this estate goes under the hammer … I swear! … I swear with all … with all my being!

ANYA [*Calmer and happier.*] Dear Uncle … oh, I feel better already … you're so good – so sensible, you're so clever. I feel much happier. No more worrying.

FIRS [*Enters.*] Leonid Andreyevich, may the Lord forgive you, have you no fear before God … when are you going to your bed?!

GAYEV Now – this minute. You go, Firs, I can undress myself for once. Enough for now, my children, off to bed. We'll talk about it tomorrow, eh? [*He kisses them both.*] You know, you're talking to a man of the eighties – oh, I've had to suffer for my convictions … the peasants don't love me for nothing. It's all in the point of view, d'you see? You've got to know your peasant … know how to –

ANYA Uncle, you're doing it again!

VARYA Uncle dear, do stop!

FIRS Leonid Andreyevich!

GAYEV All right, I'm going … I'm coming! Right, to bed. Off the cushion, into the middle. Pot the white … [*He goes. FIRS shuffles after him.*]

ANYA Dear Uncle. I feel better now. Not that I want to go to Yaroslavl, I'm not a bit fond of the old lady. Still, I've stopped worrying, bless him.

VARYA We must get some sleep. Ah, I know what I wanted to tell you. While you were away … it was so nasty and unnecessary. As you know there's hardly anyone left in the old servants' quarters … well, only Polya and Yevstignei and old Karp … anyway, they've been letting the waifs and strays in to sleep, naturally I haven't objected. And then, bless me, there's all this gossip! I'm supposed to have said they were to be fed on nothing but peas because I'm so mean – can you imagine? Of course I knew who was at the bottom of it – "Come on, Yevstignei" I said "let's have it out, you

old fool" … Anushka? Anushka? She's asleep! Come
on, darling … come to bed … come along …

[*She leads ANYA off. In the distance the sound of a*
shepherd's pipe. TROFIMOV, crossing, sees the girls.]

Ssh, don't wake her, she's asleep!

ANYA I'm tired … what are all those little bells … Mama
… Uncle?

VARYA Come along, my love.

[*They go. Sunshine floods the nursery.*]

TROFIMOV Anya! Light! Life! First flower of spring!

Act Two

[*A field. An overgrown wayside shrine, some old tombstones, and a bench. Visible, the road to* GAYEV's *estate. To one side, tall poplars bordering the cherry orchard. In the distance telegraph poles and the outline of a town. Sunset.* CHARLOTTA, YASHA *and* DUNYASHA *sitting on the bench. Close by,* YEPICHODOV *plays the guitar.* CHARLOTTA, *in an old peaked cap, has taken her shotgun from her shoulder and is adjusting the strap.*]

CHARLOTTA [*Musing.*] I wonder – how old am I? Without papers you can't tell. I think of myself as young. All that travelling from fair to fair with Father and Mama … we were good … fine performances … I did the leap of death – 'salto-mortale'! … so many tricks! And then when they died, being looked after by the German lady … being educated … thanks to her I am a governess. But who am I? From where do I come? Who were my parents – were they even married? Who knows? [*She takes a cucumber from her pocket and eats it.*] I know nothing.
  [*Pause.*]
How I should wish to talk with someone. But who? Who is there? I have no-one.

YEPICHODOV [*Plays the guitar and sings.*] "What do I care for worldly pleasure, What do I care for friend or foe …" The playing of the mandoline is very consoling.

DUNYASHA [*Powdering her nose.*] It's not a mandoline, it's a guitar.

YEPICHODOV Not to a man in love. To a man who is mad with love it is a mandoline. [*He sings.*] "If only that

37

my heart were warmed, By her returning passion's flame …"

[*YASHA joins in.*]

CHARLOTTA Dreadful … ach … you sound like hyenas on a wet night!

DUNYASHA [*To YASHA.*] You've been abroad, you're lucky.

YASHA [*Yawns, lights a cigar.*] I am, who's arguing?

YEPICHODOV Absolutely. I mean to say … abroad, everything's been sorted out long ago.

YASHA Yes, take my word for it.

YEPICHODOV I'm a mature person. I read … I've read any number of books. Remarkable books. But there's no guidance. Nothing to tell you. Should one? I mean … live? Or shoot oneself. So to speak. I carry it with me all the time. Just in case. [*He produces his revolver.*]

CHARLOTTA There … finished. [*She puts the gun over her shoulder.*] I go. You … Yepichodov … yes, very clever man … frightening too – the women fall over themselves for you, eh? Brrr! [*She moves off.*] These clever boys – so stupid. Who can I talk with? No-one. I am quite alone. Who am I … why am I? Who knows. [*She strolls off.*]

YEPICHODOV Strictly speaking, and absolutely on the point, I have to say, as far as yours truly is concerned, fate seems concerned to treat me with no mercy whatsoever. I feel like a tiny boat. Buffeted. In a storm. If I'm mistaken then why, when I woke up this morning, was there a huge fat spider sitting on my chest, as big as this. [*He makes a fist.*] Sitting. Right here. Looking at me. Again, I go to pour myself a glass of kvass,° and what do I see, waving at me through the bottle? A cockroach. An object of remarkable repulsiveness.

[*Pause.*]

Have you read 'The History of Civilisation' by the
English historian, Buckle?°

   [*Pause.*]

Could I, perhaps, have a few words with you, Avdotya
Fyodorovna?°

DUNYASHA Go on, then.

YEPICHODOV I would very much prefer it to be alone.

DUNYASHA [*Embarrassed.*] Oh all right. Only would you go
and get me my little cape out of the cupboard? I'm a
bit cold.

YEPICHODOV Very good, Ma'am. I'll fetch it. I know, now,
what to do with this. [*He pats his revolver, takes his
guitar and goes off, playing it.*]

YASHA "One foot in the Cowpat!" Between you and me,
he's a total idiot.

DUNYASHA I hope to Heaven he *doesn't* shoot himself.

   [*Pause.*]

I don't know what's the matter with me, I'm so nervy!
I suppose it's being here since I was little, I've got out
of the way of being a peasant. I mean, look at my
hands – white as white, like a lady's. I'm frightened of
everything, I'm all tender and delicate now, sort of
noble really…. Yasha if you deceive me I don't know
what I'll do my nerves won't stand for it!

YASHA [*Kisses her.*] Little pumpkin. Still, we must behave
ourselves, mustn't we? I'm not very keen on girls who
make fools of themselves.

DUNYASHA But I love you so much! You're educated! You
can talk about anything!

YASHA [*Pause. He yawns.*] Ye-es. In my experience, once a
girl's fallen in love, she loses all sense of shame.
[*Pause.*] If there's one thing I enjoy, it's lighting up a
cigar in the open air. [*He listens.*] Somebody's coming.
It's them.

   [*DUNYASHA embraces him impetuously.*]

Go back along this path here, as though you'd been for a swim. I don't want you bumping into them, they'll think we're keeping company, heaven forbid!

[*DUNYASHA snuffles quietly.*]

DUNYASHA It's the smoke ... from your cigar ...

[*She goes. YASHA remains sitting by the shrine. Enter LYUBOV ANDREYEVNA, GAYEV and LOPAKHIN.*]

LOPAKHIN You must make a decision. Time won't wait. It's quite simple. All I need is a straight answer. Will you agree to lease your land for building dachas or not? All I need is one word, yes or no ... just one word!

LYUBOV Who on earth's been smoking these disgusting cigars? [*She sits.*]

GAYEV Very good, you know ... the railway. Having it so close. Into town for lunch ... yellow into the middle – here we are again, just in time for a frame or two....

LYUBOV Oh, no hurry.

LOPAKHIN Look, please ... just one word. I must have an answer!

GAYEV [*A snub.*] Who?

LYUBOV [*Looks into her purse.*] Hardly a thing. Plenty yesterday. There's poor Varya giving everyone soup that's mostly milk and feeding the servants dried peas for their dinner, and here am I, spending away ... [*She drops her purse, scattering gold coins.*] there, you see? I'm throwing them everywhere!

YASHA Allow me, Madame. [*He picks them up.*]

LYUBOV Thank you, Yasha. Why did we go out to lunch? That vile restaurant of yours with the dreadful music, and tablecloths smelling of carbolic. Why did we eat so much? Why did you drink so much, Lenya? Talking your head off as usual. Who wants to hear about the Seventies? They're not interested in the Decadents! Who on earth, in that restaurant, is interested in the

Decadents – my dear, I'm sorry, but it's true! The waiters have no idea what you're talking about!

LOPAKHIN Absolutely!

GAYEV [*Waving a hand.*] I know, I know…. I'm hopeless, you don't have to tell me…. [*To YASHA, irritably.*] What the devil are you up to, under my feet?

YASHA Trying to keep a straight face.

GAYEV Either he goes, or I go.

LYUBOV Off you go, Yasha.

YASHA [*Trying not to grin.*] Oui, Madame! [*He gives her the purse and goes.*]

LOPAKHIN You know who's after your land? Deriganov. He's a rich man. They say he's coming to the auction himself.

LYUBOV Where did you hear that?

LOPAKHIN In town.

GAYEV We're expecting some family money from Yaroslavl. I'm not sure when –

LOPAKHIN How much?

GAYEV The amount's uncertain.

LOPAKHIN A hundred thousand? Two?

GAYEV Hardly that. Ten or fifteen thousand … we'll be grateful for that.

LOPAKHIN Forgive me, but with all due respect you're the most frivolous, unbusinesslike people I've ever met in my life. Here you are, being told in plain Russian that the estate is being sold over your heads, and you don't seem to understand a word.

LYUBOV But what are we to do? Tell us what to do.

LOPAKHIN I've told you. I keep telling you. I never stop telling you…. I repeat the same thing, day after day. The cherry orchard, and the rest of the land must be leased out for building dachas, it must be done now, at once … the auction's almost on us, there's no time! For God's sake say you agree … here – this minute!

The moment you say yes, I can lay my hands on money for you, as much as you want. No more debt … you'll be saved …

LYUBOV Dachas? Summer visitors? Forgive me, Yermolai Alexei, but we couldn't! Not in the cherry orchard! So … ugly!

GAYEV I entirely agree. Out of the question.

LOPAKHIN I shall fall down or start screaming in a minute! It's no good, I can't stand any more … [*To GAYEV*.] and you're nothing but an old woman!

GAYEV [*A snub*.] Who?

LOPAKHIN You heard me – a useless old woman!
    [*He makes to go*.]

LYUBOV No, please – don't go! My dear, stay, please … I beg of you. We'll think of something, surely?

LOPAKHIN Think of what?

LYUBOV Please stay. Don't go. At least it's cheerful when you're here.
    [*Pause*.]
I keep expecting something awful to happen. It's as if the house was about to fall on our heads …

GAYEV [*Miles away*.] Red in the corner … pot into the middle …

LYUBOV … as a punishment …

LOPAKHIN Punishment … for what?

GAYEV [*Eats a sweet*.] I'm supposed to have eaten my fortune away in sweets for a start. [*Laughs*.]

LYUBOV Oh, for my sins. I've always spent money like a lunatic. I married a man who only knew how to get into debt … killed himself drinking champagne … oh, how he drank! I fell in love with someone else – God, what a misfortune! We had an affair. It was a punishment … don't you see? Losing my little boy. Here, right here in that awful river … it all happened together … so you see … like a terrible blow to the

head, I … he was drowned. My little boy. I went away,
I went abroad, what could I do, I meant never to come
back, ever. Never, never see that river again, I went, I
didn't know what I was doing, where or who I was.
And he followed me. You know who I mean … it was
cruel of him. I bought the villa in Menton because of
him – he was ill. Three years I nursed him … day and
night, it wore me out, my soul seemed to die within
me. In the end I had to sell, to pay our debts, I came to
Paris, he came after me and he … he … it was so cruel.
He robbed me. And then left. For another woman. I
even tried to poison myself … shameful … stupid! And
then suddenly I wanted to come home … home, to
Russia! To my little girl! [*She wipes away her tears.*]
Dear Lord … pity me! Forgive us our sins … don't
punish me any more. [*She pulls a telegram from her
pocket.*] This came. Today. From Paris. He wants me
to forgive him. To go back. [*She tears up the telegram
and then turns her head, listening.*] Is that music?

Gayev That's our famous Jewish orchestra. Don't you
remember, four violins, flute and double bass.

Lyubov It still exists? We must have them here sometime
… we'll arrange an evening.

Lopakhin [*Listens.*] I can't hear anything. [*He sings,
quietly.*] "So long as you pay, The Germans will play,
And turn our Ivan, To a Frenchie Jean"° … [*He
laughs.*] I saw a good play at the theatre last night.
Very funny.

Lyubov I don't suppose it was in the least funny. Why
watch plays? Why not look at yourselves more often?
The grey lives you live … all the unnecessary talking
you do.

Lopakhin True. I suppose our existence here does seem
pretty meaningless.

  [*Pause.*]

My father was a peasant. An idiot. Understood nothing … taught me nothing – all he ever did was to get drunk and beat me with a stick. Am I any better? I doubt it. Just as much of an oaf and an idiot. What have I learnt? My handwriting's so bad I'm ashamed to let people see it, it's worse than a pig's.

LYUBOV You need a wife, my friend.

LOPAKHIN Yes, that's true.

LYUBOV What about our Varya? She's a good girl.

LOPAKHIN Yes.

LYUBOV Good, plain background, never stops working but much more important … she loves you. And you've liked her for a long time now.

LOPAKHIN Well, I don't mind. She's a nice girl.

    [*Pause.*]

GAYEV I've been offered a job in a bank. Six thousand a year, did you hear about it?

LYUBOV That's not for you. Stay as you are.

    [*FIRS enters. He carries an overcoat.*]

FIRS On with this, if you please, sir. It's getting damp.

GAYEV You're an old nuisance, my friend.

    [*But he puts on the overcoat.*]

FIRS It's no good. Off he goes this morning … never told me.

    [*He inspects his master.*]

LYUBOV You're getting old, Firs!

FIRS What can I do for you, Madam?

LOPAKHIN She says you've aged!

FIRS I've lived a long time, that's why! They were marrying me off before your dear Papa was born. [*He laughs.*] I remember the day the freedom° came. I was head valet by then … I didn't want no freedom, I never took it, I stayed with my Master. Oh, they was all singing and carrying on because they was free … what it all meant nobody knew.

LOPAKHIN Yes, so much better in the old days. At least you got your back flogged!

FIRS [*Not hearing.*] That's it! The peasants belonged to the masters, and the masters belonged to the peasants, you knew where you were. Now it's all topsy-turvy, can't make any sense out of it.

GAYEV Be quiet, Firs. I've got to go into town tomorrow. Someone promised to introduce me to a General who might agree to lend money on a note.

LOPAKHIN Don't waste your time. If you get it, you won't be able to keep up the interest.

LYUBOV Nonsense! There isn't any General.

[*Enter TROFIMOV, ANYA and VARYA.*]

GAYEV Ahh … the children!

ANYA Here you are, Mama.

LYUBOV Come … my own darlings! [*She embraces ANYA and VARYA.*] If you knew how much I loved you. Sit here, next to me.

LOPAKHIN Ah, the wandering student° … never far from the ladies.

TROFIMOV Oh keep it to yourself!

LOPAKHIN He'll be fifty soon and he's still a student.

TROFIMOV I wish you'd stop.

LOPAKHIN What's the matter with you? What are you getting upset about?

TROFIMOV Stop provoking me.

LOPAKHIN [*Laughs.*] All right. On one condition. Tell me what you think of me.

TROFIMOV My opinion of you? Very well, since you ask. You're a wealthy man, Yermolai Alexeyevich. Before long you'll be a millionaire. And just as the predatory beast that devours everything in its path is a necessary part of the metabolism of nature, so you too have your place and function.

[*Everyone laughs.*]

Varya Pyotr° … stick to the planets, you're on safer ground.

Lyubov No – where were we yesterday?

Trofimov What was it about?

Gayev We were talking about pride.

Trofimov We talked for a long time yesterday, but we didn't get anywhere. You saw something mystical in man's pride in himself. Perhaps you're right, from your point of view, but if we look at the matter simply, what have we to be proud of as a species? Physiologically we're not at all well constructed, what is more, in the majority of cases human beings are coarse, unintelligent, and often deeply unhappy. We should stop admiring ourselves and get down to work.

Gayev Why? We die in the end just the same.

Trofimov Who knows? And what does it mean, die? It may be that man has a hundred senses, that with death only the five senses known to us perish, and the other ninety-five remain alive.

Lyubov You're so clever, Petya!

Lopakhin [*Ironic.*] Oh, absolutely amazing!

Trofimov We do advance, mankind is going forward. All that is beyond our reach today will be known, will be understood. But we must work! We must support those who seek the truth! How many people, here in Russia, commit themselves to serious work? The vast majority of the intelligentsia that I know do nothing, they're incapable! They patronise their servants, treat the peasants like animals, but do they read seriously, study properly? They call themselves intelligentsia and sit about *talking* about science, understanding nothing of art … all they do is pull heavy faces and philosophise about abstractions and weighty matters. And all around them, under their very eyes, people starve! Live on foul scraps … sleep thirty, forty to a

room in damp, sour beds full of lice ... what chance of
any privacy let alone decent standard of morality?
What are all these fine conversations for? Except to
blind ourselves to the truth under our own noses.
Where are the reading rooms everyone was talking
about? Where are the creches? You won't find them,
outside the covers of uplifting novels. In real life, what
do we see? Dirt, squalor ... and barbarism. When I
listen to these intense conversations ... when I sit and
watch people with sincere expressions on their faces,
do you know what it does? It frightens me. I think
we'd do a lot better to shut up.

LOPAKHIN You know, I get up at four o'clock every
morning. I work from morning to night handling
money, my own and other people's. And I can tell you,
there aren't many decent – very few honest people.
When you work you soon find that out. Sometimes,
when I can't sleep, I get to thinking ... 'Dear God ...
look at what you've given us. Endless forests ... fields
... horizons ... so much!' We should be giants, living in
such a country.

LYUBOV Giants? Who wants giants ... much too
frightening. Leave those in the fairy tales.

[*YEPICHODOV crosses, playing his guitar.*]

Ah, Yepichodov ...

ANYA Yepichodov ...

GAYEV There goes the sun, ladies and gentlemen.

TROFIMOV Yes. Gone.

GAYEV Oh nature ... divine nature ... burning with your
eternal light ... wonderful ... indifferent – you in
whom Life and Death unite ... you, in whom the
power of life and the power of destruction –

VARYA Uncle, dear!

ANYA Uncle, you're doing it again!

TROFIMOV I should pot the yellow into the middle pocket.

47

GAYEV Silence. I say no more.

[*Silence, except for FIRS muttering. A sound, as if from the sky, far off … like a string breaking. A sad sound which dies away.*]

LYUBOV What was that?

LOPAKHIN I don't know. Perhaps a cable in a mineshaft breaking … whatever it was it was a long way off.

GAYEV Might have been a bird. A heron perhaps.

TROFIMOV Or an owl …

LYUBOV [*Shudders.*] Eerie …

[*Silence.*]

FIRS It was the same before the disaster. An owl hooted and the samovar° never stopped singing.

GAYEV What disaster?

FIRS The freedom.

[*Pause.*]

LYUBOV We must go in, friends, it's getting dark. [*To ANYA.*] My darling, what is it? … There are tears in your eyes! What is it, child? [*Embraces her.*]

ANYA Nothing, Mama. Nothing.

TROFIMOV Who's that?

[*A MAN appears. He wears a white, shabby cap and a coat. He is slightly drunk.*]

MAN Will I get to the station this way?

GAYEV Yes, just follow the path.

MAN Thank you very much, sir. Much obliged. [*He coughs.*] Wonderful weather, eh? [*He declaims.*] "My friend, my brother … my tired, suffering brother … how they groan on the Volga, the men … haul away" … [*To VARYA.*] Mademoiselle … a few kopeks for a hungry fellow Russian … [*VARYA pulls away, frightened.*]

LOPAKHIN That's enough of that!

Lyubov [*Alarmed.*] Here ... take this ... [*She dives into her purse.*] ... oh, I haven't any silver – it doesn't matter, here's a gold coin.

Man Obliged to you ... very grateful ... very ... [*He goes.*] [*Laughter.*]

Varya [*Nervous.*] I'm going in. Oh Mama, darling, how could you? There's nothing for the servants to eat at home, and you give him a gold coin!

Lyubov What's to be done, I'm a fool! You shall have all I've got when we get home. Yermolai Alexeyevich, you'll lend me some more?

Lopakhin Of course, Ma'am.

Lyubov Time to go, ladies and gentlemen. And Varya, darling, since we've more or less promised you in marriage ... congratulations!

Varya Oh Mama, please don't make jokes.

Lopakhin Get thee to a monastery, Ohmelia° ...

Gayev Time for billiards – d'you know, it's so long since I had a game my hands are quivering.

Lopakhin Ohmelia ... O Nymph in thy prayers remember me!°

Lyubov Come along, everyone ... time for dinner.

Varya He really frightened me. My heart's still beating.

Lopakhin Let me remind you, ladies and gentlemen, that all of this is about to be sold! The auction is on the twenty-second! The cherry orchard is going to be sold ... in two weeks! Think about it! Think!

[*They go, except ANYA and TROFIMOV.*]

Anya [*Laughs.*] We're on our own, thanks to the man who frightened Varya!

Trofimov She's afraid we'll fall in love, that's why she follows us about all the time. Love! All this narrow-minded concern with petty illusion, can't she understand that we're above all that? We must be free of the small, the pointless ... throw away the banal in order to go forward in freedom and happiness. We must go forward! Forward to that bright star on the horizon … forward, friends, together … don't be left behind!

ANYA [*Throws up her arms.*] How well you speak!

[*Pause.*]

It's been wonderful here today.

TROFIMOV Yes, the weather's amazing.

ANYA What have you done to me, Petya? Why don't I love the cherry orchard as I used to? I loved it so dearly I thought there was no better place on earth.

TROFIMOV The whole of Russia is an orchard. The earth is vast … beautiful … full of marvellous places.

[*Pause.*]

Think of it, Anya. Your father, your grandfather … all your forebears were serf owners – they owned living souls! Can't you see them … all those people – behind every cherry, every leaf, every tree-trunk a human being watching you – can't you hear their voices? To own living souls! It's changed you, perverted you, all of you … your forefathers, your mother, your father, your uncle … you don't even notice – you're living on credit at the expense of others … people who you don't even allow beyond your front hall! We're two hundred years behind the times … at least! We still have nothing – no attitude to our past, all we do is sit about philosophising, and drinking vodka and complaining that we are bored. How can we begin to live in the present if we don't redeem the past … come to terms with it? There is only one way. By suffering. By work. By extraordinary effort … by unceasing toil. Try to understand that, Anya.

ANYA This house hasn't been ours for a long time now. Believe me, I shall go. I give you my word.

Trofimov Yes. Throw the keys down a well and leave. Be as free as the wind.

Anya Oh, you say it so wonderfully!

Trofimov Believe me, Anya, believe me! I'm not thirty yet, I'm young, I'm still a student, but I've been through so much already. I go hungry in the winter, I'm sick, anxious, I'm as poor as a beggar – if you knew where I'd been, what I've seen! Even so … all the time … every moment of the day and night I'm filled with the most wonderful and inexplicable premonitions. I have such visions … such premonitions of happiness. Anya, I feel it here … now …

Anya [*Dreamily.*] The moon's rising.

    [*Moonlight. YEPICHODOV can be heard, playing the same sad song.*]

Varya [*Off.*] Anya! Where are you?

Trofimov Yes … the moon's rising!

    [*Pause.*]

Here comes happiness. I feel it coming closer and closer … I hear its footsteps … I feel its presence … if not for us … what does it matter if we never know it, never see it … others will!

Varya [*Off.*] Anya! Anya, where are you?

Trofimov Varya again! Unbearable!

Anya Let's go down to the river, it's lovely there.

Trofimov Yes, come on!

    [*They go.*]

Varya [*Off.*] Anya!

Act Three

[*The drawing room – connected by an archway to the ballroom. Evening, the chandelier is lit. The sound of the Jewish band. The grand-rond is being danced.*]

PISHCHIK [*Off.*] Promenade à une paire!
>   [*They enter the drawing room: PISHCHIK and CHARLOTTA, TROFIMOV and LYUBOV ANDREYEVNA, ANYA with a MAN from the post office, VARYA, weeping and wiping her eyes as she dances with the STATION-MASTER, DUNYASHA and A. N. OTHER.*]

PISHCHIK Grand rond, balancez! … Les Cavaliers à genoux, et remerçiez vos dames!
>   [*FIRS, in a tailcoat, enters with soda water. PISHCHIK and TROFIMOV return, the dance is over.*]

It's the blood pressure, d'you know. I've had a couple of turns … strokes. Makes dancing difficult – but you know the old saying … when you're up with the pack you've got to wag the tail, whether there's a bark left in you or no. Mind you, I'm as strong as a horse! My old father, God rest his soul … he loved a joke … he used to say that the ancient stock of the Semyonov-Pishchiks was descended from Caligula's horse° … the very horse! [*He sits.*] Trouble is … what about the hay? How do the oats get paid for? When the dog's hungry he dreams of meat all the time. [*He drops off, snores, wakes himself up.*] I'm the same. Money, money … I never think of anything else.

TROFIMOV Perhaps there's something in it.

PISHCHIK Eh?

TROFIMOV You do look a bit like a horse, come to think of it.

PISHCHIK Very noble beast. A horse'll fetch a good price.
    [*The sound of billiards. VARYA appears under the arch.*]

TROFIMOV Aha … Madame Lopakhina! Madame Lopakhina!

VARYA And Aha to you … the 'flea-bitten gent'!

TROFIMOV Why not? I'm proud of it.

VARYA Will you listen to that! [*She gestures towards the music.*] Who on earth's going to pay for it! [*She goes.*]

TROFIMOV If you took all the energy you waste looking for money to pay your debts, and used it on something worth while, you could change the world.

PISHCHIK What is it the philosopher says? … You know the fellow I mean … great philosopher … intellect – very famous … Nietzsche! He says it's all right. To forge banknotes.

TROFIMOV Have you read Nietzsche then?

PISHCHIK Not what you might call read him … Dashenka tells me that sort of – fact is, I'm in such a state I might be tempted. I've got till the day after tomorrow. To find three hundred and ten. Roubles. I've managed to lay my hands on a hundred and thirty – hullo, where is it, where's it gone? I've lost it … my money's gone … I've lost my money! I've lost – oh, here it is … dropped down the lining. Phew! Brings you out in a cold sweat!
    [*Enter LYUBOV ANDREYEVNA and CHARLOTTA IVANOVNA.*]

LYUBOV [*Humming a Caucasian° dance tune.*] Why is Leo taking so long? It's so late … he can't still be in town – [*To DUNYASHA, crossing.*] – Dunyasha – don't forget the musicians … make sure they're offered tea. [*DUNYASHA goes back the way she came.*]

TROFIMOV Perhaps the auction was cancelled.

LYUBOV Hardly the time for a band ... or for a ball. ... Never mind. [*She sits, humming quietly to herself.*]

CHARLOTTA [*Hands PISHCHIK a pack of cards.*] Pick a card. Now shuffle. Thank you, mein Herr Pishchik. Ein, zwei, drei ... et hoopla! Look in your right pocket ...

PISHCHIK The eight of spades! I'll be damned! Unbelievable!

CHARLOTTA [*To TROFIMOV, a pack of cards in her hand.*] Quick, what's the top card?

TROFIMOV Oh, I don't know – the Queen of Spades.

CHARLOTTA Voilà! [*To PISHCHIK.*] What's the top card?

PISHCHIK The ace of hearts.

CHARLOTTA Et voilà! [*She claps her hands, the cards disappear.*] Marvellous weather we're having! [*A mysterious voice answers, as from under the floor.*] Oh indeed, a beautiful day, Madame. What an attractive man! [*Again the voice.*] You too, Madame!

THE STATION-MASTER [*Applauds.*] Madame the Ventriloquist ... bravo!

PISHCHIK Unbelievable ... can you imagine ... unbelievable! Charlotta Ivanovna, you're an enchantress. ... I'm falling in love with you ...

CHARLOTTA You? Love? "Guter Mensch aber schlechter Musikant" as we used to say ... the instrument's there, but can it play?°

TROFIMOV [*Slaps PISHCHIK's shoulder.*] You old hack, eh?

CHARLOTTA Attention please. One more trick. [*She takes a rug from a chair.*] Here's a fine rug ... here you are, ladies and gentlemen, a fine rug for sale.... [*She opens it up.*] Who wants to buy?

PISHCHIK Can you believe it ... unbelievable!

CHARLOTTA Ein, zwei, drei! [*She whisks aside the rug, and there is ANYA, who curtseys, runs to her mother and embraces her, and runs back into the ballroom. Applause.*]

LYUBOV [*Applauding.*] Bravo! Bravo!

CHARLOTTA And once more … ein, zwei, drei! [*She flips the rug aside once more, and VARYA is revealed. VARYA bows.*]

PISHCHIK [*Astonished.*] Unbelievable … unbelievable!

CHARLOTTA Ending!

[*She throws the rug over PISHCHIK, curtseys and runs off to the ballroom.*]

PISHCHIK [*Makes after her.*] You little minx! I'll catch you – [*Goes.*]

LYUBOV Still no sign of Lenya – where is he, what's keeping him so long, surely it's all over by now. Either it's happened or it hasn't, why keep us in suspense?

VARYA Uncle will buy it, of course he will!

TROFIMOV [*Sarcastic.*] Of course.

VARYA It was all arranged. Great-Aunt gave him power of attorney to buy the estate in her name and transfer the mortgage to her – she's doing it for Anya's sake! Uncle will buy it – you'll see – it's God's will!

LYUBOV It was to be in her name because she doesn't trust us. Fifteen thousand roubles – not even enough to pay the interest! [*She covers her face.*] My whole life is being decided today. My whole life … !

TROFIMOV [*Teasing VARYA.*] Madame Lopakhina!

VARYA The perpetual student!° The university's thrown him out twice!

LYUBOV Darling, don't be cross – why be upset? If you want to marry Lopakhin, marry him. He's an interesting man, a good man. Of course if you don't want to, then don't. Nobody's forcing you.

VARYA I know, Mother. But all this joking. I take it seriously. He is a good man. I do like him.

LYUBOV Then marry him my dear. What are you waiting for?

VARYA Darling Mama, I can hardly propose myself! For two years everyone's been talking about it … everyone but him! He either says nothing, or he makes jokes. I know what it is … he's building up his business, his head's full of affairs, there's no time for me. If I had the money, a hundred roubles even, I'd leave everything and go into a convent!

TROFIMOV The life of bliss!

VARYA Being a student, of course, he has to show us all how clever he is. [*More gently.*] Oh Petya … you're looking older … you're beginning to lose your looks … [*She wipes her eyes, turns to LYUBOV ANDREYEVNA.*] It's only that I can't bear the thought of having nothing to do. I must be working, Mama.

YASHA [*Enters, stifling laughter.*] Yepichodov's broken a billiard cue … [*He goes.*]

VARYA What is Yepichodov doing here? And who on earth allowed him to play billiards? I simply do not understand people … [*She goes.*]

LYUBOV You mustn't tease her, Petya. She's unhappy enough as it is.

TROFIMOV She's always interfering. All summer she's been after Anya and me, frightened we're going to fall in love! Why should she think that? It's so trivial! We're above all that.

LYUBOV And I must be beneath it, I suppose. Oh, where is he? What's happened? Is it sold or not? I can't conceive of such a disaster, it's all so unbelievable, I'm lost, I can't think … I could scream out loud … I shall do something stupid … help me, Petya! Say something – quick, do something … say something to me … please … help me …

TROFIMOV What does it matter? What difference does it make if the estate's sold today or not? There's no turning back … it's over … finished and done with long ago. Stop worrying. And stop deceiving yourself –

dear lady, for once in your life look at the truth and face it.

LYUBOV The truth? What truth? You can see it. You seem to know where it lies. I seem to have lost my vision … I see nothing. All these important problems that you settle so courageously … my dear boy, could it not be because you're young! There hasn't been time to face any of these problems! You look ahead so bravely.… Why is it that you don't see, … don't expect terrors … isn't it because you haven't lived? Life is still hidden from your eyes! You're bolder, yes … more honest … deeper than we are, but my dear … put yourself in our shoes. Can't you show just a tiny bit of generosity … be a little less judging? I was born here. My father and my mother – and my grandfather … they all lived here before me. I love this house. I can't imagine my life without the cherry orchard. If it's to be sold, then I go with it! [*She kisses him on the forehead.*] My child was drowned here. [*She weeps.*] You're a dear, kind boy. Try to understand.

TROFIMOV You know I do. With all my heart.

LYUBOV You shouldn't say such things. Not like that. [*As she takes out her handkerchief, a telegram falls from her pocket.*] If you knew the weight on my heart today. The noise here … my soul trembles at every sound … I tremble all over, but I can't go to my room, the silence terrifies me, I can't be on my own! Don't judge me, Petya. I love you like a son. Of course you can have Anya … but … my dear boy … when are you going to finish your degree? You do nothing.… Fate seems to throw you about from place to place … it's all so odd! It's true … yes? And you really must do something about that beard – it's neither one thing nor the other. [*Laughs.*] You look ridiculous!

TROFIMOV [*Picking up the telegram.*] I'm not trying to look beautiful … what do looks matter?

LYUBOV [*Takes the telegram from him.*] It's from Paris. I get one every day. He wants me to forgive him … to go back. I should, he needs me, he's hopeless on his own – oh, don't look like that, Petya … I know, I know, but what am I to do? He's ill! He's all on his own, there's no-one to look after him. Who'll see he gets his medicine, stop him getting into trouble? Why shouldn't I say it, why should I hide it … I love him. I love him! He'll drag me down, I know he's a millstone, I know that. But I love him. I can't be without him. [*She presses his hand.*] Please Petya, don't say anything … don't judge. Just … nothing … please … mmm?

TROFIMOV [*Upset.*] Forgive me. I'm sorry … but – for heavens' sakes, he's robbed you – well hasn't he?

LYUBOV No, no, please … no, don't … don't say it … [*She covers her ears.*]

TROFIMOV He's a parasite, everyone knows it but you, nothing but a petty, worthless –

LYUBOV And you are twenty-seven years old and you still behave like a schoolboy.

TROFIMOV Oh, never mind me!

LYUBOV Grow up! You should be old enough by now to understand what it means to be in love … don't you know what it means, aren't you capable of love? You should fall in love – love someone! Yes! Yes! Forget about all this purity … you're nothing but a prig … a freak – a monster!

TROFIMOV [*Horrified.*] What are you talking about? … I don't know what you mean!

LYUBOV "I'm above love"! Are you insane … no, I'll tell you what you are … Firs knows … you know what he'd call you … a 'good for nothing'.… Not having a mistress … at your age … it's unnatural!

TROFIMOV You … can say this? I can't believe what I'm
hearing … no … please … awful … [*He stumbles off
towards the ballroom.*] you, of all … [*He returns.*] it's
over between us! [*He goes.*]

LYUBOV Petya, wait! I was only joking … Petya!

TROFIMOV [*Off.*] Finished … finished! [*The sound of steps
on stairs, and then someone falls. ANYA and VARYA
shriek, and then burst out laughing.*]

LYUBOV What is it, what's happened? [*As ANYA runs on,
laughing.*]

ANYA Petya's fallen downstairs! [*She runs off again.*]

LYUBOV Oh Petya, you funny boy!

[*THE STATION-MASTER walks to the centre of the
ballroom, begins to read from "The Sinner" by Alexis
Tolstoy.*°]

THE STATION-MASTER To plangent cry of lute and cymbal,
By festooned pillar, by flowered pool,
Hist to the name of Pontius Pilate,
He who embodies Roman rule.
But soft among the clamorous clatter,
Who walks with face sublime, serene?
A man, a man is come among us –

[*A waltz begins. The others dance and he is forced to
stop. TROFIMOV, ANYA and LYUBOV
ANDREYEVNA enter from the hall.*]

LYUBOV Come Petya – my dear innocent, come, let's dance
… say you forgive me …

[*She dances with TROFIMOV. ANYA and VARYA
dance together.*]
[*FIRS enters, putting his stick by the door. YASHA enters
and watches the dancing.*]

YASHA What's up, Grandpa?

FIRS No, not too good. In the old days we had generals
and admirals, not post-office clerks and
station-masters … even they don't want to turn up

60

now! No ... my legs is going. Now my old Master –
your Mistress's grandfather ... what he used to do
when we was ill was give us sealing-wax. Never mind
what was wrong with us, what we got was
sealing-wax. I been taking it every day for the last
twenty year, perhaps that's what keeps me going.

YASHA Give it up then, sooner the better.

FIRS I'll see you off ... good-for-nothing. [*Goes on
muttering.*]

> [*TROFIMOV and LYUBOV ANDREYEVNA dance,
> first in the ballroom and then in the drawing room.*]

LYUBOV Merci. Let's sit down a minute. [*She sits.*] Ooh,
I'm tired!

ANYA [*Enters, agitated.*] There's a man in the kitchen
saying that the cherry orchard has been sold!

LYUBOV To whom?

ANYA He didn't say. He's gone. [*She dances with
TROFIMOV into the ballroom.*]

YASHA Just some stranger ... some old man gossiping out
there.

FIRS And Leonid Andreyevich still not back. He's only
got a light coat on, it's a mid-season coat, he'll catch
his death, you see ... these young people!

LYUBOV I'm going to die, this very minute. Yasha, go and
find out who bought it.

YASHA The old man's gone ... he went! [*He laughs.*]

LYUBOV [*Only slightly annoyed.*] What are you laughing
about ... what's so funny?

YASHA Yepichodov ... you know what they call him ...
"One foot in the ... ah ... mud."

LYUBOV [*To FIRS.*] But Firs, where will you go, if the
estate is sold?

FIRS Where you tell me to, that's where I'll go.

LYUBOV Why are you looking like that? Are you ill? Go to
bed!

FIRS Oh yes … [*He grins.*] and who's going to do the waiting and look after everybody? There's only me for the whole house.

YASHA [*Aside.*] Lyubov Andreyevna, could I have a word? I was wondering if Madame would be going back to Paris, and if I could have the honour of coming too. [*He lowers his voice.*] I'm sure Madame understands, you can see for yourself. They're all so rough and uneducated, there's no sense of moral refinement, and it's so boring, the food's uneatable, that old man wandering about muttering to himself, look, take me with you … please!

PISHCHIK [*Enters.*] May I have the pleasure, enchanting lady … a turn at the waltz … [*They dance.*] Enchanting lady … alas, all the same I must beg a 180 roubles of you … I must … [*They dance.*] just a 180 little roubles … [*They dance into the ballroom.*]

YASHA [*Sings quietly.*] "And will you, can you understand, The anguish of my heart" …

[*In the ballroom a figure in a grey top hat and check trousers waves her arms and leaps about.*]

VOICES Bravo … Charlotta Ivanovna!

DUNYASHA [*Stops to powder her nose.*] The mistress said I could join in the dancing because there aren't enough ladies … ooh, it's made me all dizzy, my heart's pounding. Oh, and you'll never guess what the post-office clerk said to me just now, Firs Nicolayevich … took my breath away!

FIRS What?

DUNYASHA He said … "You … are like a flower."

YASHA [*Yawns.*] Ignorant peasants! [*He goes.*]

DUNYASHA Like a flower. I absolutely love it when people use words like that. I'm very sensitive. I take it all in …

FIRS Oh, you'll get taken in all right.

YEPICHODOV [*Enters.*] [*To DUNYASHA.*] There you are. You keep moving away, as if I were some sort of insect. [*He sighs.*] Oh … life!

DUNYASHA What do you want?

YEPICHODOV You could be right, of course. [*Sighs.*] But if one is to look at it from that point of view, if you'll allow me to express myself this way … forgive my frankness but you've driven me utterly into a state of mind … it's of no account, I know what fate has in store for me, every day there's a new … believe me, I'm well acquainted with – but I don't let it … as you can see, I'm smiling – Avdotya Fyodorovna, you gave me your word – !

DUNYASHA Oh go on, leave me alone. We can have a talk later. I'm all in a dream. [*She plays with her fan.*]

YEPICHODOV No … please … as you see … [*He cackles with laughter.*] I'm perfectly … I can even … [*He sighs.*] I just make light of it.

VARYA [*Enters from the ballroom.*] Semyon, what are you doing here, you don't belong here, why haven't you gone, you really are – [*To DUNYASHA.*] – Dunyasha, off you go! [*To YEPICHODOV.*] First you go and break a billiard cue – who said you could play billiards? Now I find you walking all over the drawing room as if you were a guest!

YEPICHODOV Permit me to venture to assert…. Who do you think you are, asking me to vacate the premises?

VARYA I'm not asking you, I'm telling you. All you do is wander about doing nothing. What on earth we employ a clerk for heaven knows, you never do any work.

YEPICHODOV [*Offended.*] The only people who are entitled to judge whether I work, or wander about, or eat or play billiards are my elders and betters … in other words, those in a position to do so.

VARYA How dare you speak to me like that! You dare! Are you telling me that I'm not … that I don't know what I'm talking about? Get out of here! This minute … go on!

YEPICHODOV [*Cowering.*] I must ask you to express yourself with more delicacy.

VARYA [*Beside herself.*] Out … this minute … out!
[*He goes to the door. She follows him.*]
One foot in the Cowpat! Out! Get out of my sight!
[*He goes.*]

YEPICHODOV [*From behind the door.*] I shall complain …

VARYA [*Grabs FIRS's stick.*] Oh you will, will you? Come on, we'll see about that … come on … are you coming?
[*She raises the stick. LOPAKHIN enters, dodging the blow.*]

LOPAKHIN Thanks very much!

VARYA [*Sarcastic.*] My pleasure!

LOPAKHIN Don't mention it, Ma'am. I've had worse welcomes.

VARYA I daresay. Did I hurt you?

LOPAKHIN No, no … just a bump the size of an ostrich egg, nothing to worry about.

VOICES [*Off.*] He's back! Yermolai Alexeyevich is here! Lopakhin's arrived!

PISHCHIK [*Enters.*] Here you are, my dear fellow … he's here, everyone…. [*He embraces LOPAKHIN.*] Ah, cognac – you've been enjoying yourself too, I see … we've been having a fine time!
[*Enter LYUBOV ANDREYEVNA.*]

LYUBOV Yermolai Alexei … is that you? Why so long? Where is Leonid?

LOPAKHIN Leonid Andreyevich is here too, he's just arrived.

LYUBOV Well? Well? Tell me! What happened? Did the sale take place?

LOPAKHIN [*Confused, afraid to reveal his joy.*] The auction
ended just before four. We missed the train ... we had
to wait till half past nine. [*He groans.*] Ohh! Sorry, my
head's going round ...

　　[*GAYEV enters. He carries parcels in his right hand,
　　wipes away tears with his left.*]

LYUBOV Lenya! What is it, Lenya? [*Breaking down.*]
Quickly, for God's sake!

GAYEV [*Waves a hand in her direction, and hands his
parcels to FIRS.*] Here, take these will you ... some
anchovies and pickled herrings from Kuch ... I haven't
eaten all day ... what I've been through!

　　[*The sound of billiards.*]

YASHA [*Off.*] Seven and eighteen!

　　[*GAYEV cheers up at the sound.*]

GAYEV Ouf, I'm tired! ... come and help me change, Firs.

　　[*He goes off through the ballroom, followed by FIRS.*]

PISHCHIK What happened at the sale? Tell us!

LYUBOV Has it been sold ... the cherry orchard?

LOPAKHIN Yes, it's been sold.

LYUBOV Who to? Who bought it?

LOPAKHIN I bought it.

　　[*Pause.*]

　　[*LYUBOV ANDREYEVNA is stunned. She steadies
　　herself against a table. VARYA takes the keys from her
　　waist, throws them onto the floor in the middle of the
　　drawing room and walks out.*]

Yes! I bought it! Just a minute, ladies and gentlemen,
my head's spinning, I can't think straight! [*He laughs.*]
When we got to the auction, Deriganov was already
there. Leonid Andreyevich had only the fifteen
thousand, of course, and Deriganov bid thirty at once,
over and above the mortgage. I see how the land lies so
I come in at forty ... he goes to forty-five ... I bid
fifty-five. That's how it went ... him bidding in five

thousands, me in tens … well, at last it's over. I paid 90,000 over the mortgage, and it was mine.

[*With a great shout of laughter*.] Good God! The cherry orchard's mine! Tell me I'm drunk … dreaming … out of my mind … [*He stamps his foot several times*.] Don't laugh at me!

If my father and grandfather could see me now. My God, if they could rise from their graves! If they could see me, their son, Yermolai, who was illiterate … beaten … who ran about barefoot in the snow … that Yermolai has bought this estate … !

I've bought this estate. The most beautiful thing in the whole world. Where my father and grandfather were serfs. Where they weren't allowed even into the kitchens. I must be dreaming … I'm asleep … it's something I'm imagining … I only think it's true … it can't be … just a dream … imagined in the dark….

[*He picks up the keys and smiles tenderly*.] She threw them down … the keys. To show she wasn't mistress here any more. [*He jingles the keys*.] Well, no matter.

    [*He hears the band tuning up*.]

Hey … you in there … play! I want to hear you! Everybody – come and see Yermolai Lopakhin wielding his axe on the cherry orchard … down they come – down comes the cherry orchard … watch the trees come crashing down! We're going to build dachas for our children … and our children's children – they'll see a new life here – music … play!

    [*The musicians play. LYUBOV ANDREYEVNA sits, collapsed, in a chair, weeping bitterly*.]

Why? Why didn't you listen to me? My poor, dear lady, it's done … over. Too late. [*He breaks*.] Why must it be like this? Why can't we get the suffering over, done with, quickly! Why can't we change … finish with all the mess and misery in life!

PISHCHIK [*Takes his arm, speaks low.*] She's crying. Come into the ballroom, we'll let be, eh? Come ...

LOPAKHIN What's happening – where's the music? Everything must be as I say! [*With irony.*] Here comes the new landlord ... the new owner of the cherry orchard! [*He bangs into a small table, nearly overturning the candelabra.*] That's all right ... I can pay for it. [*He goes, with PISHCHIK.*]
   [*LYUBOV ANDREYEVNA, alone, weeps. The music plays softly.*]
   [*ANYA and TROFIMOV enter hurriedly. ANYA goes to her mother and kneels beside her. TROFIMOV remains standing by the door to the ballroom.*]

ANYA Mama ... oh Mama, are you crying? Dear, kind, sweet Mama ... oh I love you, my beautiful Mama ... God bless you! It's gone ... our cherry orchard is gone ... but don't cry. You have your life in front of you ... you're still your dear, loving self. We'll go away from here, darling – let's go away at once ... we'll go! We'll plant a new orchard ... much more splendid ... and when you see it you'll understand, Mama, and happiness ... a deep, quiet happiness will bathe your heart in its glow, like the warmth of the evening sun and you'll smile again. Come ... you'll see, dearest ... come!

Act Four

[*The nursery ... without curtains or pictures. A few
remaining pieces of furniture are stacked in a corner, as if
ready for sale. A forlorn air of emptiness about the room.
Suitcases, bundles and bags piled near the door. The other
door is open and* ANYA's *and* VARYA's *voices are heard.*
LOPAKHIN *stands, waiting.* YASHA *holds a tray with
champagne and glasses.* YEPICHODOV *is tying up a large
trunk. The sound of many voices, off.*]

GAYEV [*Off.*] Thank you, friends ... thank you ...

YASHA It's the people from the village, here to say
goodbye. Salt of the earth in my opinion, Yermolai
Alexei. A lot of thickheads, though, eh?
  [*The voices die away.* LYUBOV ANDREYEVNA *and*
  GAYEV *enter through the hall. She is pale and
  tremulous.*]

GAYEV There was no need to give them your purse, Lyuba.
You shouldn't have done that, you really shouldn't!

LYUBOV I couldn't help myself! I couldn't help it!
  [*They go out.*]

LOPAKHIN [*Calls after them.*] Please! A farewell glass! I
managed to get a bottle at the station ... I didn't think
of it in town. Please! No? [*He moves away from the
door.*] If I'd known I wouldn't have bothered.... I can't
drink on my own. [*YASHA carefully places the tray on
the table.*] Here, you ... Yasha ... have a drink – at
least you can have one.

YASHA To those that are going! And to those who are
staying behind! [*He drinks.*] This isn't real, you know
– it's not real champagne.

LOPAKHIN Cost me eight roubles the bottle.

[*Pause.*]

Devilish cold in here.

YASHA They didn't light the stoves today … no point, we're leaving! [*He laughs.*]

LOPAKHIN What's so funny?

YASHA Nothing, I feel cheerful that's all.

LOPAKHIN October already, and still fine outside. Good building weather. [*Looks at his watch, calls out.*] The train leaves in forty-six minutes, ladies and gentlemen – we must leave in twenty minutes … hurry up, please.

[*TROFIMOV enters from outside, wearing an overcoat.*]

TROFIMOV It must be time to go, the horses are here. [*He calls.*] Anya, have you seen my goloshes, I can't find them!

LOPAKHIN I'll come on the train with you as far as Kharkov, I'm spending the winter there. It'll be good to get back to work, I've spent far too long around you lot doing nothing. Hate not working, don't know what to do with my hands. They flop around as though they don't belong to you.

TROFIMOV We'll be gone any minute, you can get back to your valuable labour.

LOPAKHIN Drink?

TROFIMOV No thank you.

Varya! Why is she so upset? … [*He inspects the goloshes.*] They're not even mine!

LOPAKHIN I sowed three thousand acres of poppy last spring, God, what a sight, you should have seen it. Take the money … I cleared 40,000, I won't even notice the difference. Come on, what's the matter with you? Why turn your nose up? Look, don't expect fine words, I'm just a peasant.

TROFIMOV The son of a peasant. And I'm the son of a chemist, and neither has the least bearing.

[*LOPAKHIN pulls out his wallet.*] Don't! If you

offered me two hundred thousand I wouldn't take it! I'm free of all that ... all the things you crave, all you rich people – and poor people.... All these things have no power over me. They are no more than thistledown floating in the air as far as I'm concerned. I walk past you, I do without you. Can't you understand? Humanity is on the move towards a higher truth ... towards the greatest happiness possible on this earth ... and I am in the van, in the front rank!

LOPAKHIN Get there, will you?

TROFIMOV I'll get there.

[*Pause*.]

I'll get there. Or point the way. Others will get there.

[*In the distance, the sound of an axe hitting a tree*.]

LOPAKHIN Time to go. Goodbye, my friend. We've no opinion of each other – well, what does it matter, life slips by as we talk. When I'm working my head off, day after day, I do get the feeling ... my thoughts move from one thing to the other ... yes, there is a feeling, a sense of meaning.... I feel I know why I exist. How many people in Russia, my friend, have any purpose in their lives ... eh? Still, the world circulation ... er ... circulates just the same. As they say. I hear Leonid Andreyevich has a job at the bank ... six thousand a year. He'll never stick it – too much like hard work.

ANYA [*At the door*.] Mama says, would you please ask them not to cut the trees till we've gone?

TROFIMOV My God! Have you no tact at all? [*Exits through hall*.]

LOPAKHIN All right, all right ... these people ... [*Follows him*.]

ANYA Have they taken Firs to hospital?

YASHA I imagine they have, I told them this morning.

ANYA [*To YEPICHODOV, who crosses the ballroom.*]
Semyon Panteleyevich, could you make sure that Firs
was taken to hospital?

YASHA How many times do I have to repeat it – I told
Yegor this morning!

YEPICHODOV I'm bound to say … in my considered opinion
the venerable Firs has reached an irreparable state of
dilapidation. I can only conclude that he approaches
the moment when … when he should meet his
forefathers and I envy him! [*Drops a case on a hatbox,
squashing it.*] There! You see? I knew that would
happen! [*Exits.*]

YASHA Both feet in the Cowpat!

VARYA [*At the door.*] Has Firs been taken to hospital?

ANYA Yes he has.

VARYA Then why didn't they take the letter for the doctor,
it's still here!

ANYA I'll send someone with it. [*She goes.*]
[*DUNYASHA, in and out with the luggage, hangs about.*]

VARYA [*Off, from the next room.*] And where's Yasha?
Tell him his mother's here, and she wants to say
goodbye!

YASHA [*Waves his hand.*] Oh, she'll only annoy me.

DUNYASHA [*Now that she and YASHA are alone.*] Please
Yasha, at least look at me. You're going, aren't you …
you're leaving me … [*She weeps, throwing her arms
about his neck. He detaches himself.*]

YASHA What is there to cry about?
[*He helps himself to champagne.*] I'll be in Paris in a
week! We'll be on the express by tomorrow, and away,
I can't believe it … Vive La France! I've seen enough of
this place – nothing but ignorant peasants – I've had
enough. No need to cry – show some elegancy.

DUNYASHA [*Pulls herself together at this hint, looks into a
mirror and powders her nose.*] You'll write to me?

From Paris? You know I love you ... I've loved you,
Yasha ... loved you – oh, so much! Ah, I'm so delicate
... I have such soft, tender feelings –

YASHA Shut up, they're coming.

[*He hums, pretending to be busy with the luggage.
LYUBOV ANDREYEVNA enters with GAYEV, ANYA
and CHARLOTTA IVANOVNA.*]

GAYEV We must go soon ... almost time. [*With a hard
look at YASHA.*] There's a sort of peasant smell in
here ... who's smelling of herring?

LYUBOV Another ten minutes and we'll be getting in the
carriages ...

[*She looks round the room.*]

Goodbye dear ... darling old grandfather house. One
more winter ... one more spring and you'll be gone ...
they'll have pulled you down. What haven't these old
walls seen. [*Kisses ANYA fiercely.*] Oh my love, my
treasure, you're glowing ... your eyes are shining like
diamonds! Are you pleased ... are you happy?

ANYA Oh yes, Mama ... yes! A new life is about to begin!

GAYEV [*Gaily.*] That's right! Everything's fine! Think how
worried ... how miserable we all were ... before the
cherry orchard was sold. When it was all over ... done
... no going back ... we all calmed down, we even
cheered up. I'm an old hand at banking, no problem
there ... a man of finance, eh? ... Yellow into the
centre pocket, eh? You look better already, Lyuba ...
no, no, you do ... no doubt about it.

LYUBOV Yes, it's true. My nerves are better.

[*She takes her hat and coat.*]

I'm sleeping. Yasha ... my things. It's time to go. [*To
ANYA.*] My little girl, we'll see each other soon,
darling. I'll stay in Paris for a while on the money your
great-aunt sent ... thank God for Yaroslavl – however,
it won't last forever.

ANYA Don't stay too long. Come back soon – you will, won't you, Mama? I'll study and pass my exams, then I'll be able to work and help you. We'll read to each other. [*Kisses her mother's hands.*] We'll sit together in the long autumn evenings and read and read, lots and lots of books, and a whole new world will open up for us. ... [*Dreamily.*] Come back soon, Mama ...

LYUBOV I shall, my love. [*Embraces her.*]

[*CHARLOTTA sings to herself. LOPAKHIN enters.*]

GAYEV You see, Charlotta's happy – she's singing.

CHARLOTTA [*Picks up a bundle, holds it like a baby.*] Bye, bye, my little one. ... [*The bundle 'cries'.*] There, there, be good.... [*More 'cries'.*] Ah, my pretty one, my darling boy! [*She throws the bundle down.*] I shall need a new job. You will find me one – I must exist.

LOPAKHIN Don't worry, Charlotta Ivanovna, we'll find something for you.

GAYEV Everyone's leaving us. Varya's going ... nobody wants us any more.

CHARLOTTA There's nowhere to live in town ... move on, I suppose. Ah well, never mind.

[*PISHCHIK enters.*]

LOPAKHIN Here comes the natural phenomenon.

PISHCHIK [*Breathless.*] Ooh ... ooh dear ... let me get my breath back ... oof ... my dear friends ... some water please ...

GAYEV After a loan, I suppose. Good day to you, sir ... I'm off. [*He goes.*]

PISHCHIK So long since I've called, lovely lady. ... [*He sees LOPAKHIN.*] Aha, you're here ... glad to see you, my dear fellow ... you're a genius ... here ... take this ... [*He hands LOPAKHIN some money.*] four hundred roubles ... I still owe you eight hundred and forty....

LOPAKHIN [*Gestures in surprise.*] I must be dreaming ... who did you get it from?

PISHCHIK Wait ... I'm hot ... an astonishing thing! These people turned up, on my land. Englishmen. They've found this sort of white clay ... [*To LYUBOV ANDREYEVNA.*] four hundred for you ... dear, beautiful, wonderful lady that you are ... the rest later. [*He finishes the water.*] A young man on the train was just telling us about some great philosopher who advises jumping off roofs – "Just jump!" he says, and that settles it. [*Astonished.*] Unbelievable! Water!

LOPAKHIN Englishmen?

PISHCHIK They've taken a twenty year lease. On the land. With the clay. And now, forgive me, I must dash ... first the Znoikovs ... then Kardamonov ... I owe them all money.... [*He drinks.*] Your good health! ... I'll look in again on Thursday.

LYUBOV But we won't be here! We're just leaving for town ... tomorrow I shall be on the train – for Paris!

PISHCHIK Eh? What? Town? [*He looks about, sees the packing.*] Ah ... oh ... I see. All the furniture ... the cases. I see. Well. Ah well ... never mind. Unbelievable. [*He blows his nose.*] Never mind ... very interesting, these Englishmen ... never mind. Unbelievable. I wish you every happiness.... God will protect you ... never mind ... everything comes to an end in this world. [*He kisses LYUBOV ANDREYEVNA's hand.*] And when you hear I've gone, and a horse trots by, give me a thought, eh? Perhaps you'll even say "Hullo, there goes a horse. I knew an old fellow like that once ... what was his name? Semyonov-Pishchik – yes, that was it, God rest his soul." Wonderful weather ... yes ... [*He goes off, in great confusion, but returns.*] Dashenka asked to be remembered to you! [*Goes.*]

LYUBOV We might as well go. Just two worries ... there's poor Firs who isn't well.... [*She looks at her watch.*] We could wait another five minutes ...

ANYA Mama, Firs has been sent to hospital – Yasha saw to it this morning.

LYUBOV Ah! What about Varya? She's used to getting up early and working. She's like a fish out of water with nothing to do.... I hate to see the poor girl so pale and miserable and in tears half the time.

[*Pause.*]

You know very well, Yermolai Alexeyevich, that I hoped to see her married to you ... everything seemed to point that way. [*She whispers to ANYA, who makes a sign to CHARLOTTA, both leave.*] She loves you, and you're fond of her and I don't know, I just don't know why you seem to avoid each other. I don't understand it!

LOPAKHIN Not sure I do myself. It's odd. If it's not too late, let's settle it here and now. Let's settle it – basta! Mind you, without you here, I don't think I'd ever do it.

LYUBOV Splendid, I'll call her now. It'll only take a minute.

LOPAKHIN I've even got champagne for the occasion. Oh, someone's been drinking ... [*YASHA coughs.*] or I should say, guzzling.

LYUBOV Wonderful. We'll go – Yasha, allez, allez! I'll get her ... [*She crosses, calls.*] Varya, will you come here? No ... leave all that! [*She goes.*]

LOPAKHIN [*With a glance at his watch.*] Yes. [*Pause.*]

[*Laughter and whispering, off. VARYA enters. She begins to sort out the luggage.*]

VARYA [*After a pause.*] Funny, I can't find it ...

LOPAKHIN What are you looking for?

VARYA I ought to know, I packed it myself.

[*Pause.*]

LOPAKHIN Where are you off to now, Varvara Mihailovna?°

VARYA Me? To the Ragulins. I said I'd go and help them, as a sort of housekeeper.

Lopakhin Over at Yashnevo? That's about seventy versts,° isn't it? [*Pause.*] Well, life in this house seems to be over.

Varya [*Poking about among the luggage.*] Where on earth is it? Yes, that's the end of it – it's all over, the life here …

Lopakhin And I'm off to Kharkov … on this train, as a matter of fact. A lot of business there. I'm leaving Yepichodov in charge outside.… I've taken him on.

Varya Well, that's your affair.

Lopakhin Last year it was already snowing by now, remember? Here we are, still sunshine. Pretty cold though. Three degrees of frost.

Varya Really? I didn't look.

    [*Pause.*]

Anyway, our thermometer's broken.

    [*Pause. Then a voice calls "Yermolai Alexei!"*]

Lopakhin [*Promptly.*] Coming! [*He goes quickly.*]

    [*VARYA sits on a bundle and begins to cry. LYUBOV ANDREYEVNA enters discreetly.*]

Lyubov Well?

    [*Pause. VARYA pulls herself together and wipes her eyes.*]

Lyubov [*Gently.*] We must go.

Varya I know, Mama darling. I shall be able to get to the Ragulins tonight, if we don't miss that train.

Lyubov [*Calls.*] Anya, get your coat!

    [*ANYA enters, followed by GAYEV and CHARLOTTA. GAYEV wears a warm overcoat with a hood. SERVANTS and COACHMEN assemble and YEPICHODOV busies himself with the luggage.*]

Our journey begins!

Anya [*Joyfully.*] Yes … we begin!

Gayev Friends … dear good friends! As I leave this house, as I bid farewell for the very last time, allow me to express my feelings. How can I be silent, how can I

refrain from expressing my emotions as I take my leave
… feelings which at this moment fill my whole –

ANYA Uncle!

VARYA Uncle please, no!

GAYEV [*Crushed.*] Double the yellow … middle pocket … silence!

[*TROFIMOV enters, followed by LOPAKHIN.*]

TROFIMOV Well now, ladies and gentlemen! Time to go.

LOPAKHIN Yepichodov – my coat.

LYUBOV Just one more minute. I just want to sit … just for another minute. It's as if I'd never really looked at this house before. Never looked at the walls … never looked at the ceilings … never really looked. And now I can't get enough … I'm filled with such longing … such love …

GAYEV I remember sitting on this window sill, when I was six. It was the Feast of the Holy Trinity and I sat right here, watching Father walk to Church …

LYUBOV Have they taken everything?

LOPAKHIN It looks like it. [*To YEPICHODOV.*] Just the same, keep an eye on things for me.

YEPICHODOV [*Hoarsely.*] Don't worry, Yermolai Alexei.

LOPAKHIN What's the matter with your voice?

YEPICHODOV I drank some water and … and swallowed something.

YASHA Ignoramus!

LYUBOV When we've gone, there won't be a soul left here …

LOPAKHIN Not until the spring.

[*VARYA pulls an umbrella from a bundle. LOPAKHIN dodges, as from a blow.*]

VARYA What's the matter, why must you – you know I wasn't … the thought never even –

TROFIMOV Into the carriages, ladies and gentlemen, the train will be here any minute.

Varya Here they are, Petya! Your goloshes. Next to the suitcase. Oh, they look so old and worn … [*She cries.*]

Trofimov [*Putting them on.*] Please everyone … we must go …

Gayev [*Trying not to break down.*] Ah yes … the train … the station … croisez to the middle, white to centre pocket …

Lyubov Yes … let's go.

Lopakhin Are we all here? Nobody left behind? [*He locks the door to the left.*] I'd better lock up, with things left in the house. Right. Off we go.

Anya Goodbye, old house! Goodbye, old life!

Trofimov To the new life! [*He leaves with ANYA.*]
[*VARYA looks round, and leaves without hurrying. YASHA and CHARLOTTA go off, with the dog.*]

Lopakhin Till the spring then. For now it's goodbye … time to go, ladies and gentlemen. [*He goes.*]
LYUBOV ANDREYEVNA and GAYEV are left. Now at last they can embrace. They fall into each other's arms and sob quietly, afraid of being overheard.]

Gayev Oh my sister … my beloved sister …

Lyubov Oh my dear … my gentle, beautiful orchard! … my life … my youth … my happiness … goodbye … farewell!

Anya [*Off, cheerful.*] Mama!

Trofimov [*Off, excited.*] Ah-hoo!

Lyubov One last look. The walls … the windows … how Mother loved to walk in this room …

Gayev My sister … my sister!

Anya [*Off.*] Mama!

Trofimov [*Off.*] Ah-hoo!

Lyubov We're coming! [*They go.*]
[*The sounds of doors being locked, and of carriages leaving. Silence. The hollow sound of an axe on a tree.*]

[*Footsteps. FIRS appears from the door on the right. He enters in white waistcoat and jacket, with slippers. He looks unwell. He tries the handle of the middle door.*]

FIRS Locked. They've gone. [*He sits down on the sofa.*] They've forgotten about me. Never mind. I'll sit here for a while. And he won't have put on his fur coat, Leonid Andreyevich ... he'll be wearing that light coat ... I should have made sure ... these youngsters. [*He mutters unintelligibly.*] Life's gone by ... it's as if I'd never lived. [*He lies down.*] I'll lie down for a while. No strength left ... all gone ... nothing left ... nothing ... you old good-for-nothing ... [*He is still.*]

[*There is a distant sound, as though from the sky, like the sound of a breaking string, dying away with a melancholy sound. Silence. The sound of an axe striking a tree, far off in the orchard.*]

RESOURCE NOTES

Who wrote *The Cherry Orchard* and why?

Chekhov, the man

Anton Chekhov was born in 1860 in the Crimea region of southern Russia. His grandfather had been a serf. In Russia at that time serfs had in effect been slaves to the landowners, working as peasants whose services could be sold by their masters. Chekhov's grandfather had bought his freedom, and his family's. Chekhov's father struggled to make a living as a grocer, but he was not successful, and in 1875 he was declared bankrupt and fled to Moscow.

When Chekhov himself went to Moscow in 1879, he became a medical student and began writing to make some money. He initially sold all kinds of material (jokes, anecdotes and short stories) to humorous magazines. He qualified as a doctor when he was 24, and continued to work in medicine for much of the rest of his life – often stating that as a practising doctor he was able to use his observations of people as raw material for stories and plays. By 1885 he had begun to write more serious stories, and in 1888, at the age of 28, he was awarded the Pushkin Prize for Literature.

In 1884, at the age of 24, he had already begun showing symptoms of tuberculosis; and in 1889, the year in which his elder brother, Nikolai, died, he became bitterly depressed: he was distressed by his brother's death, shaken by the poor reception given to his first full length play, *The Wood Demon* (which had been taken off after only three performances), and dispirited by his own deteriorating health. In the years that followed he made occasional visits abroad (including trips to Italy and to Nice on the French riviera) in the hope of improving his health.

In 1898 he saw the actress Olga Knipper in a production at the Moscow Art Theatre. Soon afterwards he wrote to his closest friend, 'Were I to stay in Moscow, I would fall in love with her'. By autumn of the following year they had become lovers; and in 1901 they married. Three years later Olga played the part of Lyubov Andreyevna Ranyevskaya in the first production of *The Cherry Orchard*.

In spite of his ill health and the apparent failure of *The Wood Demon*, he continued writing, producing the four major plays by which he is best known (*The Seagull*, *Uncle Vanya*, *Three Sisters* and *The Cherry Orchard*) in the last eight years of his life. In July 1904, six months after the Moscow opening of the first production of *The Cherry Orchard*, Chekhov was staying in a hotel at the German spa resort of Badenweiler, when he suffered two heart attacks and died. He was forty four.

✦ *Activity*

Although the above is only a very brief summary of Chekhov's life (and *The Cherry Orchard* is certainly not directly auto-biographical) there are ways in which any writer's work reflects their personal, social and cultural experience. Before reading any further, discuss:

• What is there in the play that appears to reflect Chekhov's own life? This is a question you may want to return to after reading the section below on Russia in the nineteenth and early twentieth centuries.

Chekhov as a writer

When Chekhov began writing he did so in order to supplement his meagre income as a medical student. He wrote in order to live, although he continued to practise as a doctor for most of his life, and was convinced that 'my studies in medicine have had a serious impact on my literary activities. They considerably broadened the scope of my observations and enriched me with a knowledge whose true value for me as a writer only a doctor can appreciate.'

He was enormously prolific as a writer. The short stories he wrote throughout his life were very popular in his day, and covered an extraordinary range. As Michael Frayn wrote in 1988:

> The skits and spoofs with which he began his literary career while he was still a medical student matured seamlessly into stories of the most exquisite restraint and insight. ... Even if he had never written a single line for the theatre he would still be one of the most marvellous writers ever to have lived.
>
> ('Introduction' to *Plays by Anton Chekhov*)

Several of these 'short stories', most notably *The Duel*, should perhaps be thought of as short novels – not only because of their length, but also because of the richness and depth of characterisation, and the interplay of complex ideas. The themes of these stories include:

- problems of communication between people;
- conflicts between people's desires and the reality of their situation;
- tensions between characters arising out of changing social circumstances.

The stories are frequently distinguished by:

- non-judgmental attitudes towards the characters, particularly concerning their sexuality (which was remarkably liberal, given the society in which Chekhov lived);
- a recognition that there could be a variety of approaches to difficult issues;
- a celebration of the difference between people;
- an ability to characterise men and women from very varied social backgrounds and with very different attitudes (for example: bishops and peasants; shepherds and businessmen; upper class gentlemen and actresses; dull, ageing lechers and cold, calculating predators; committed revolutionaries and dilettantes), and to do so with great precision and economy.

Initially Chekhov had difficulties in making the transition from writing short stories and vaudevilles to full-length dramas. His first full-length plays – *The Wood Demon* and *Ivanov* – were failures. In 1895 he began work on *The Seagull*. 'I am actually writing a play,' he wrote at the time. 'I am writing it with pleasure, though I sin much against the conventions of the stage …' It opened in 1896 at the Alexandra Theatre in St. Petersburg. The audience hated the play; it seemed he had yet another disaster on his hands; on the opening night, Chekhov vowed never to write plays again. Fortunately, he broke his vow! *The Seagull* was soon performed again – this time in Kiev, where it was very successful. By 1898 this play had had its first foreign production. It has remained very popular, and is still frequently performed throughout the world. He went on to write *Uncle Vanya* (effectively a reworking of *The Wood Demon*), *Three Sisters* and *The Cherry Orchard*. At the time of his death he was working on a new play which was to be about two men (who had at different times in their lives passionately loved the same woman) finding themselves together on an Arctic exploration. Unfortunately none of Chekhov's work on this last play has been discovered.

◆ *Activity*

Many of the short stories' themes and characteristics are also present in *The Cherry Orchard*. Note some specific examples of each.

Chekhov's Russia

◆ *Activity*

a Before reading this section any further, note all the references to historical events in the play. Use the term 'historical' very loosely, to include major events which would have affected most Russians, and local events which would have affected the characters who appear in the play.

b Note all the references in the play to other cultures. Charlotta, for example, frequently refers to her childhood;

Lyubov to her trips to France. What might this tell you about Russian society at this time?

c Discuss what else the play tells you about Chekhov's perceptions of contemporary Russia. Using the play text as a resource, make a list of observations, noting all the information you can about the social and political conditions in which the play takes place. The following list can be used a starting point:

- wealthy families had servants, including maids and footmen, some of whom would have stayed with the same family all their working life;
- wealthy Russians were free to travel throughout Europe;
- it was possible for a widow to conduct an open affair;
- it was possible for someone who had been born into a peasant family to make a great deal of money.

Now add at least ten further observations of your own.

The social and political situation

Russia was, and is, a vast country (its land mass nearly twice the size of the USA; more than fifty times larger than the United Kingdom). Russia at this time was ruled by a Tsar (sometimes spelt 'Czar' – the word comes from the Roman 'Caesar'), an absolute ruler who exercised far greater power than the English monarchy had been constitutionally allowed since the English Civil Wars (1642–1649). In spite, or maybe partly because of, its vast size, industrialisation occurred much later in Russia than in Western Europe. In 1861, Tsar Alexander II passed an Act 'freeing' Russia's twenty two and a half million peasants from serfdom. Before this, serfs had been controlled by landowners (such as the family in *The Cherry Orchard*), unable to move freely, unable even to marry without their 'owner's' permission. The 'freedom' had mixed results: some left the rural estates, found work in towns, and made money; others were worse off than before. For millions of former serfs the 'freedom' resulted in a loss of security (because the landowners no longer had a legal responsibility for their workers): freedom might not have seemed to be worth much if you owned nothing and had no work. In 1901 a writer in *The Economist* (a periodical magazine published in London) asserted:

> Russia is at the parting of the ways, one eye fixed on her simple agricultural past, the other gazing forward into what the government believes will prove her great industrial future. Such times are always trying for nations, especially when they are imperfectly prepared. …

Chekhov was acutely aware of the extremes of difference between the poor and the wealthy; of the unrest in the country; the sense of imminent change; and the desperate need for continuing social and political reforms.

✦ *Activity*

Consider each of the following characters:

- Semyonov-Pishchik
- Lopakhin
- Trofimov
- Gayev
- Firs
- Lyubov

Identify lines in the play where each character reveals their attitude to change (for example, Pishchik's account of the railway going through his land). How does each of them view the various changes that are occurring in Russian society at the time of the play?

The years that followed: 1904–1917

In 1904, war broke out between Russia and Japan. Russia's humiliating defeat in 1905 unleashed a 'revolution'. Mutinies in the armed forces and civilian riots spread across the whole of Russia. Tsar Nicholas II was forced to issue an imperial manifesto that transformed the country from an absolute autocracy to a semi-constitutional monarchy in an attempt to quell the mounting unrest. However, the changes were superficial, and considerably more far-reaching reforms were needed. Famine and appalling losses in the First World War made things even worse. In February 1917, liberals and moderate socialists finally overthrew the Tsarist autocracy. In March the Tsar abdicated; he and his family were shot the following year. In November 1917, the revolutionary Bolsheviks overthrew the liberals and moderates, resulting in the establishment of a communist, *soviet* government (the beginning of the USSR).

✦ *Activity*

Imagine Trofimov twenty years older than he appears in the play. Assuming that his views did not change, how do you think he might have reacted to the changes and revolutions that occurred in Russia? Use the various speeches he makes (especially in Act 2) as the basis for your discussion.

The theatre and the world of the arts

Russia at the turn of the century was a country with a strong cultural and artistic heritage. Moscow and St. Petersburg boasted some of the most magnificent architecture in Europe. Chekhov's short stories contributed to an already rich literary tradition. Poetry, novels and short stories by Alexander Pushkin, Fyodor Dostoyevsky, Leo Tolstoy and Ivan Turgenev were highly regarded throughout the world.

In the late nineteenth century, Russia was not renowned for the quality of its theatre, however. Chekhov's disappointment at the first night of *The Seagull* resulted at least in part from a disparity between the demands of the play and the current practices of production and performance. The play had received only eight rehearsals in total and was performed in front of scenery which came out of ready-made stock. The audience might well have been expecting something much more brash – both in style and content.

Elsewhere in Europe, however, theatre was undergoing something of a revolution; a revolution which was soon to have a profound effect on Russian theatre. (The Resource Notes in the sections headed 'What type of play is *The Cherry Orchard*?' and 'How was *The Cherry Orchard* produced?' examine the nature of this theatrical revolution, and how Chekhov's work proved to be vitally important to it.)

Many of Russia's aristocratic and upper-class families maintained strong links with Western Europe, frequently visiting the great capitals. The French language was so fashionable that it was virtually the adopted language of the aristocracy. There were well-established cultural links between Paris, the newly fashionable French riviera towns and Moscow and St. Petersburg. Chekhov himself travelled to Italy, France and Germany; and he spent the last few weeks of his life in the German spa town of Badenweiler. In his last letter (to his sister, four days before his death) he wrote, 'I would like to visit Como in Italy ... and to take the steamer from Trieste to Odessa.'

◆ *Activity*

How do the different characters in the play view their own culture? Find a couple of sentences spoken by each of the following characters which give some insight into the way they feel about contemporary Russia and, in particular, Russian culture:

• Yasha
• Trofimov
• Lopakhin
• Pishchik
• Yepichodov

a Speak these lines aloud, and then create a choral montage to represent these various attitudes, using lines spoken by different characters.

b Summarise their feelings about Russia in your own words. Where possible use the events and dialogue of the play to inform your suggestions.

◆

What type of play is *The Cherry Orchard*?

✦ *Activity*

a Before reading the notes which follow, try to classify the play for yourself. What *sort* of play do you think it is? Is it a comedy? A thriller? A tragedy? A documentary drama? Is it realistic or heightened in style? A play with a moral? Or what? You don't have to squeeze it into a single 'pigeon hole'. You might, for example, say that it has comic elements, but ...

b It's also worth noting what kind of play you think it is *not*. Don't retreat from stating the obvious. If, for example, you think that whatever else it might be, it's definitely *not* a thriller, that might say something about the significance of the plot.

c Discuss how the play relates to other dramas that you're familiar with. How is it similar? How is it different? What did you expect when you first started reading it? Did it fulfil these expectations, not live up to them, or work out differently?

A controversial play

The Cherry Orchard contains no real violence, no passionate crimes, not even any really radical, political ideas, yet ever since it was first performed, people have argued about it. Here are some of the issues:

• Whether it is a light comedy about frustrated love affairs, or a domestic tragedy about a stubborn family refusing to accept that their estate is part of a rapidly changing society and that their way of life will have to change.

• Whether it is a political play, in which Lopakhin and Trofimov offer different versions of a new society, or a nostalgic celebration of old values.

• Whether Lopakhin should be played as an insensitive oaf, or an enlightened and generous entrepreneur.

- People have even disagreed about whom they see as the play's central character: Lyubov Andreyevna (Madame Ranyevskaya) or Lopakhin? Or perhaps the play does not have a central character in the normal sense? Maybe the orchard itself is a sort of central character?

Discuss some of these issues between yourselves – always referring back to the play to try to support your argument.

Comedy in *The Cherry Orchard*

Chekhov began his career as a writer by producing comic short stories, and his short vaudevilles are, by definition, comedies. It would be surprising, then, if *The Cherry Orchard* didn't contain at least some comic elements. But however much Chekhov himself insisted that it should be played 'as a comedy, even a farce at times', it is undoubtedly a play which deals with some very serious issues. (See pages 116 to 118, to explore the extent to which the play is political.)

Now think about the humour in the play, for there are numerous moments in the play which are potentially very funny. Consider the different *kinds* of comedy in the play. It's possible to identify the following:

- slapstick
- running gags
- catch phrases
- misunderstandings between characters
- farcical entrances and exits
- character and situation comedy
- bathos (deliberately anti-climactic contrast between the elevated and the common-place).

✦ *Activities*

1 Regardless of whether you find the play at all funny at this stage, identify moments when each of the above seem to be operating. The above is not a comprehensive list, and you

may be able to identify other ways in which humour works in the play.

2 Look at the following specific moments within the play:
- Yepichodov's first appearance in Act 1 (page 16);
- Lyubov telling Pishchik that she ate crocodile in Paris (page 26);
- Trofimov falling downstairs in Act 3 (page 60);
- Varya attacking Lopakhin with Firs's stick (page 64);
- Lopakhin and Varya – the near proposal (pages 76–77);
- Gayev trying to evade embarrassment by potting imaginary billiard balls (at various points throughout the play).

Using the list above as a starting point, discuss what *type* of comedy is operating in each instance.

'Laughter through tears'

Consider the scene between Lopakhin and Varya in Act 4 (pp. 76–77). Varya is expecting Lopakhin to propose to her; and perhaps the audience thinks so too. Read the scene through from Lopakhin's line 'I've even got champagne for the occasion' (p. 76) to the moment when Varya 'sits on a bundle and begins to cry' (p. 77). It is possible to play the scene in a number of different ways. But in most productions, whatever the overall interpretation of the play, the moment is deeply poignant – because it is both tragic *and* comic.

This sense of moments, of scenes, and indeed the entire action of the play, as being simultaneously tragic *and* comic is important in understanding how Chekhov works as a dramatist. The terms 'comedy' and 'tragedy' are sometimes seen as exclusive: an assumption is sometimes made that if a play is a comedy it can't be tragic; and that if it's a tragedy it can't be comic; that tragedies may have comic moments, but that tragedy and comedy are essentially separate elements. *The Cherry Orchard*, however, seems to work differently: constantly keeping tragedy and comedy in tension. Indeed it is this tension which becomes the driving force of the play. It is the poignancy and painfulness of this scene between Lopakhin and Varya which makes it potentially humorous. In his own words, Chekhov was seeking 'laughter through tears'.

✦ *Activity*

Identify other scenes where Chekhov is working in this way, which are funny (or potentially funny if the actors are encouraged to play the humour), and poignantly painful at the same time.

A naturalistic play?

The Cherry Orchard is often thought of as a naturalistic play. In Western Europe and America naturalism has become the most familiar dramatic form (so familiar, in fact, that people hardly recognise it as a dramatic form at all), but there are many others. The table on page 94 gives an indication of some of the characteristics of naturalistic drama; most of these apply equally to film and TV drama as to theatre.

This list is neither definitive nor absolute. In practice there are few stage plays that can be considered *absolutely* naturalistic, and *The Cherry Orchard* is not one of them! The reason for presenting this table here is to encourage you to think about the *form* of the play. It's not helpful to think of any theatrical form as a fixed, definitive category; better to think of naturalism as one of several *tendencies*.

The earliest forms of naturalism grew up in response to changing scientific theories. For its first exponents, naturalism had the status of a scientific project. The work of naturalists reflected Charles Darwin's (1809–1882) belief in determinism: that human beings are essentially animals whose behaviour is determined by a combination of heredity and the effect of their environment.

Naturalistic drama	Non-naturalistic drama
Actors perform their roles on stage (or on film or TV) *as if* they did not know they were being observed by an audience (or a camera); the audience is encouraged to 'forget' that they are watching a drama.	Actors acknowledge the presence of the audience (for example, through asides to the audience or talking to camera), reminding the audience that they are watching a drama.
Characters speak in familiar, 'everyday' language, with recognisable speech mannerisms.	A range of language forms might be used, including poetry, song, symbolic language.
Characters are seen to be a product of their environment; they have a history.	The prime function of a character can be other than to represent a 'real' person; for example, to represent a human quality such as greed.
Characters tend to be consistent, so audiences often speak about them as if they were real people.	Audiences are made aware of the element of performance, that the 'characters' are 'constructed'.
The passage of time is chronological, sequential; on-stage time is frequently close to 'real time'.	Not necessarily chronologically sequential – the action of the play can 'jump about' in time and space.
On-stage events give the impression of being a part of a wider 'real world' – achieved through reference to 'off-stage' events in other places and other times.	The world of the drama can be overtly fictitious (as, for example, in pantomime), allegorical or fantastical.
Set, costumes and lighting are designed and organised to create an illusion of reality.	Set, costumes and lighting are not intended to create an illusion of a 'real' world; they may be symbolic or abstract, intended to create atmosphere or mood; or virtually non-existent.
Commonly set in domestic spaces.	Frequently set in non-domestic spaces: for example, on a mythical island, in the Roman Forum or in a forest.
People and things 'stand for themselves alone'.	The characters, events, the things you see can have allegorical or symbolic meanings.

✦ *Activities*

1 Research the origins of theatrical naturalism. You will find the following books particularly useful: M. Banham (ed.), *The Cambridge Guide to Theatre*, and Edward Braun, *The Director and the Stage*.

2 Consider how much detail Chekhov gives you about the characters' lives. Note the specific references to the details of the world of *The Cherry Orchard*. In one column list all those things that occur (or have occurred) in the immediate vicinity of the estate; and in another column the references to the wider world. The following table gives you a start:

References to the immediate world of the house and the estate	References to the broader world
Cherry trees now only produce fruit in alternate years.	Cherries used to go to Kharkov.
Lopakhin was looked after by Lyubov when he was a child.	Charlotta was forever doing tricks for Anya while they were on their trip to Paris.

3 Note down the time scheme for each act. How long would each act take on stage? Within the fictional world of the play, how much time is supposed to pass?

4 Using the table above, discuss the ways in which *The Cherry Orchard* might be thought of as a naturalistic play.

5 If you have studied William Shakespeare's plays you will know that he frequently acknowledges the presence of the audience. Make a list of other plays which you consider to be predominantly non-naturalistic. Discuss whether, even in these, there are naturalistic elements.

6 There is much in *The Cherry Orchard* that can be usefully described as domestic naturalism; that is, it takes place in

and around the home, and indeed the 'home' itself is at stake. But what is there in the play that is *not* naturalistic, or would at least be difficult to play in a naturalistic style?

Symbolism in *The Cherry Orchard*

Although *The Cherry Orchard* is usually thought of as a predominantly naturalistic play, it does contain a number of non-naturalistic elements. It's as if it is straining against the limitations of naturalism, in particular in its use of symbolism. The cherry orchard itself is part of the world of the play; it is referred to throughout the play; and at one level it 'stands for itself'. But it is also a symbol; it comes to stand for more than itself, and does much more than simply locate the play in a particular kind of environment. The easiest way to see this is to consider how the different characters perceive and value it.

✦ *Activities*

1 People talk about cars, cameras and items of clothing as status symbols. Discuss what sort of a symbol the cherry orchard is for different characters in the play. How do they see its significance? You might, for example, suggest that Lopakhin sees it as an obstacle to progress; but he also sees it in other ways. Note several ways in which each of the following characters view the orchard:
    • Lopakhin
    • Lyubov
    • Gayev
    • Varya
    • Anya
    • Firs

2 Now consider how each of the characters' feelings about the orchard change during the course of the play. In diagrammatic form Lyubov's reactions might look like this:

	Act 1	Act 2	Act 3	Act 4
Lyubov's reaction	Nostalgia	Denial	Agitation	Resignation

Now make a similar table, and do the same with each of the other characters noted above. You might take the exercise one stage further and express that reaction physically, for example in a series of still images.

3 Look at the stage directions at the beginning of Act 2. How do the various elements of the set function as symbols? What might they be symbols of?

4 In Act 3, when Lopakhin finally returns from the auction and announces that he has bought the orchard, Varya throws down her keys. This incident is 'realistic', believable and perfectly understandable. Discuss how it is also symbolic.

5 Find *five* more specific moments from the play when actions can be seen *both* realistically and symbolically.

A play of action?

The Cherry Orchard is sometimes considered to be a play in which not very much happens. It may not contain violent action as such, but there are numerous moments in the play when characters reveal themselves through their actions or responses to action. Consider, for example, the moment in Act 2 when The Man appears (pp. 48–49).

✦ *Activities*

1 Read the extract aloud, then 'move' it, giving careful thought to the positioning of the characters in relation to each other.

2 Discuss each character's reaction to his appearance. How does their response develop our understanding of them?

3 Now find other moments in the play when characters are revealed through action (or response). Enact these scenes and work on them in the same way.

◆

How was *The Cherry Orchard* produced?

Although Russian theatre of the late nineteenth century was not held in particularly high esteem in the rest of Europe, the country did have a long tradition of theatre. It was known especially for satiric comedy (of which the best-known example is probably Nikolai Gogol's *The Government Inspector* of 1836), vaudevilles and burlesques (such as those one-act plays written by Chekhov), romantic comedy and melodrama. Moscow and St. Petersburg (the capital city and site of the Imperial palace respectively) both boasted several major theatres.

✦ *Activity*
Although *The Cherry Orchard* works in many ways as a naturalistic play, there is still plenty to link it to the older traditions of Russian theatre. Look at Charlotta's appearances. Make a note of what she actually does in the play. Then discuss what her function might be in the drama.

Chekhov and Stanislavski
By the 1890s, the intelligentsia who travelled widely in Europe had become very dissatisfied by the state of Russian theatre, which seemed to them to be old-fashioned and irrelevant. In 1898, Konstantin Stanislavski, a wealthy businessman and amateur actor, founded the Moscow Art Theatre. From the outset Stanislavski was determined to create a new theatre, in which naturalism could flourish and in which actors would explore their roles in depth. He developed a system for training actors that is still used today. The essence of this system is to encourage actors to observe life around them accurately and to explore the life of the character from the inside as well as the outside. Stanislavski was the first person to analyse formally the *process* of acting in any depth. He demanded that his actors explore the emotional life of the characters they were

playing; to get 'beneath the surface' of a text; and to seek out the 'emotional truth' in characters and situations. He wrote several books (the best known of which is *An Actor Prepares* (1936)) that had an enormous impact on theatres all over the world.

Chekhov and Stanislavski were very important for each other. The Moscow Art Theatre needed Chekhov: as Stanislavski wrote, 'After the success of *The Seagull* and *Uncle Vanya* the theatre could not get along without a new play by Chekhov'. And Chekhov needed the Moscow Art Theatre. Chekhov's first two full-length plays, *The Wood Demon* and *The Seagull*, had disastrous first productions at second-rate theatres, lasting only three nights and five nights respectively before being taken off. In its first production, *The Seagull* had eight rehearsals *in total*. But when Stanislavski revived it for the Moscow Art Theatre, he gave it twelve *weeks'* full-time rehearsal. This was unheard of at that time, and for financial reasons is almost impossible nowadays in the British professional theatre: lengthy rehearsal periods are very expensive.

Stanislavski's method of working was both a blessing and a curse for Chekhov: a blessing because it enabled actors to explore the characters in far more depth than had hitherto been possible; a curse because Stanislavski was wedded to naturalism, and Chekhov insisted that his plays were not straightforwardly naturalistic. The second act of *The Cherry Orchard*, in particular, is notoriously difficult to stage in a naturalistic style, and leads many designers and directors to emphasise its more symbolic qualities.

Staging *The Cherry Orchard*

Designers and directors usually work in collaboration. In mounting a production of *The Cherry Orchard* they would have to consider the mechanics of the theatre in which they would be working. If you were working on the play you might want to construct a 'realistic' set for each act, although even

today it's difficult to construct stage sets which represent
outdoors naturalistically. On the other hand you might want
a set that emphasised the more symbolic elements of the play.

✦ *Activities*

Skim through the play, noting down those stage directions that
refer to items of furniture and setting, and then:

1 Draw a diagram for each act, showing what you would place
   on stage (furniture, props, etc.) and where you would have
   entrances and exits – as if you were directing / designing a
   set for a naturalistic production of the play.

2 If you took notes about symbolism in the play (see pages
   96–97), look back at these and think again about possible
   symbolic meanings of the setting of each act. Note down
   three 'things' which seem to you to encapsulate what is most
   important in each act. This might be a list of the three most
   important items of furniture (which may or may not be
   mentioned in the text), or three things which could be used
   by the characters. It may be that in each case the orchard
   itself is one of these 'things'. Here, for example, are three
   different ways of thinking about Act 1:

	Example 1	Example 2	Example 3
1	Chairs	Nursery	Window overlooking the cherry orchard
2	Bookcase	Children's toys	Faded lace curtains
3	Luggage	Doorway to Anya's bedroom	Cherry blossom

In the first example, each of the items is mentioned in the
text and could be part of a naturalistic set. In the second
example, the nursery is mentioned in the text, as is the
doorway to Anya's bedroom, but the children's toys might

be something that a designer could add to give the sense of a nursery. In the final example, the window overlooking the orchard is in the text, the other two items are a way of trying to visualise the detail of the scene.

3 When you have made your list for each act, discuss how you would use these as the basic elements of a set in a small studio theatre space. Assume that there is very little storage space off stage and no space above the stage to 'fly' scenery.

4 Now look again at the stage directions at the beginning of Act 2, and then look at the production photographs on pages 103 and 104. Both photographs are of sets for Act 2 of *The Cherry Orchard*. The first is from Stanislavski's 1904 Moscow Art Theatre production, the second from a production at the Piccolo Theatre, Milan, directed by Giorgio Strehler (1974). Although it's difficult to see it in this photograph, the rails for the model train ran all the way round the stage. When the train was at the back of the stage, it could be seen as a representation of a 'real' train – looking small because of perspective. In the foreground, running across the front of the stage (as in the photograph) it looked quite 'unreal', impossible for an audience to see it as anything except a toy clockwork train.

a Identify the different characters in each photograph.

b Comment on the relationship between the stage directions for Act 2 and the set for the Stanislavski production.

c Both sets are highly crafted pieces of design work. Draw a diagram of the set for the Stanislavski production, adding labels to show how you think it was constructed (for example, painted backcloth, real wooden bench).

d Why do you think that Strehler chose to include a clockwork toy train in his set?

5 Other recent productions of the play have also used non-naturalistic sets to draw attention to the tension

Viktor Simov's setting for Act 2 of Stanislavski's *The Cherry Orchard*, Moscow Art Theatre, 1904.
Laurence Senelick Collection

Act 2 of *The Cherry Orchard*, directed by Giorgio Strehler, Piccolo Teatro di Milano, 1974. Photographed by Ciminaghi.

between the play's naturalism and symbolism. In the 1995 Katona József Theatre production (Budapest), branches from the cherry tree protrude into the rooms of the house; in the first act they are covered in blossom; in the third, the leaves are turning yellow brown; and in the last the branches are bare. Using the lists that you made in Activity 2 above, discuss how you might create a set for the fourth act of the play which draws on the symbolist elements of the play, and yet can still be used by actors playing the text in a naturalistic acting style. Either sketch this, or draw it as a diagram.

Chekhov in translation

There is probably a wider range of translations of Chekhov than any other Russian writer. Several different translations of *The Cherry Orchard* are currently available. The text of *The Cherry Orchard* that you have in this edition was prepared by Pam Gems, a well-established playwright whose work has been staged by the Royal National Theatre in London and the Royal Shakespeare Company. She worked from a literal translation of the play by Tania Alexander.

In Pam Gems's version, Dunyasha's nickname for Yepichodov is *One Foot in the Cowpat*. Here's a selection of other translators' versions of the nickname:

- *Million Miseries*
- *Disasters by the Dozen*
- *Simple Simon*
- *Twenty Two Misfortunes*.

The last of these is the closest to a literal translation; but *One Foot in the Cowpat* has the advantage of giving a sense to an English-speaking audience of both Yepichodov's and Dunyasha's rural lack of sophistication.

Translators of plays face a number of difficult issues. These might be summarised as follows:

- Which is more important – literal accuracy or speakability?

- Is it more valuable to have someone as a translator who knows the language, or someone who can write for actors?
- As a translator, how do you render the performance style of the original?
- As a translator, to what extent are you writing for an audience in a particular culture at a particular time?
- Is your basic priority to create a play which makes sense within the culture of the audience, or to give that audience a flavour of the *Russian* culture that Chekhov knew?
- As a modern translator of a nineteenth- or early twentieth-century play, do you have your characters speak in contemporary English, in modern English, or find something that gives a *sense* of the period?

In practice, making a good translation involves balancing these different demands successfully. The following quotations – all by writers who have worked extensively as translators – give an insight into some of the problems of translation, and how translators see their own work:

> Simon Gray went to see a play of his in Germany, and in one scene one of the main characters came on covered from head to foot in plaster. And Simon Gray turned to the director, with whom he was watching this play, and said 'What the hell is going on? Why is he covered in plaster?' And the director said, 'It says in the text – "He comes on completely plastered."'
>
> (Ranjit Bolt)

> When I translate a play my real concern is to try to follow the author's intentions as closely as possible. First of all to understand the author's intentions, then to reproduce them, and to achieve the same effects that are achieved in the original, particularly with regard to working out where the author wants the audience to laugh, and trying to make them laugh in those places, which is one of the most difficult aspects of it.
>
> (Christopher Hampton)

The whole process of translating, seems to me very much like actually writing the original play. I mean, you've somehow got to put yourself back in the position the writer was in, where the thing was in his head, before he actually got it down on paper. And you've got to get these characters speaking in English instead of the original language. It feels rather like writing your own stuff.

(Michael Frayn)

A new version of a classic is a link in a chain. Why the chain? In order to connect. And I should like, with special pleading, to speak for playwrights being given the job of making new translations ... playwrights may be able to contribute something of their craft to acting versions of foreign classics.

(Pam Gems)

(The last of the above quotations is from Pam Gems's introduction to her version of *Uncle Vanya*; the others are all from *Royal National Theatre Platform Papers - 1. Translations*, published by the Royal National Theatre in 1992.)

◆ *Activity*

Look at the following short extracts – all versions of the same moment from near the beginning of Act 2 – and compare them with Pam Gems's version (p. 38). On the basis of these extracts, and using the above list of questions, discuss:

a how you think each of these translators ordered their priorities;

b which you like best, and why.

1

CHARLOTTA	How shockingly these people sing! Fie! Like jackals howling!
DUNYASHA	(*To Yasha*) What happiness it must be to visit foreign lands!
YASHA	Yes I quite agree with you. (*He yawns and lights a cigar.*)
YEPICHODOV	That goes without saying. Everything abroad has attained a full complexion.
YASHA	It certainly has.
YEPICHODOV	I am a well-read man, I have studied various remarkable books, but I cannot make out the trend of my preferences. I don't know whether I should live or, speaking bluntly, shoot myself ...

(Kathleen Cook, Progress Publishers, Moscow, 1973)

2

CHARLOTTA	The awful way these people sing – ugh! Like a lot of hyenas.
DUNYASHA	(*To Yasha*) You're so lucky to have been abroad though.
YASHA	Yes, of course. My sentiments precisely. (*He yawns, then lights a cigar.*)
YEPICHODOV	It stands to reason. Abroad everything's pretty comprehensive like. Has been for ages.
YASHA	Oh definitely
YEPICHODOV	I'm a cultured sort of person and read all kinds of remarkable books, but I just can't get a line on what it is I'm really after. Shall I go on living or shall I shoot myself, I mean?

(Ronald Hingley, Oxford University Press, 1964)

3

CHARLOTTA   *Ach, mein Gott*, they sing like goats, these people.

DUNYASHA   (*To Yasha*) Admit it though, you're very fortunate to have been abroad.

YASHA   (*Yawning*) If you like. I agree with you. (*Relights his cigar.*)

YEPICHODOV   I agree too. Abroad they've been a century ahead for years.

YASHA   Took the words right out of my mouth. (*Yepichodov takes a revolver from his waistband, stares at it for a moment, then places it experimentally in his mouth. Removes it.*)

YEPICHODOV   I'm a man of learning, you know. Oh yes, I've read a good many difficult books, I just can't seem to find my way forward. To be or not to be, really ...

(Trevor Griffiths, Faber and Faber, 1977)

✦

How does *The Cherry Orchard* present its subject?

✦ *Activity*

What do you think *The Cherry Orchard* is about? What *is* the subject of *The Cherry Orchard*? What are its central themes? Discuss these questions in groups, and then write a sales pitch for the play, as if you were trying to get a Hollywood producer interested in making it into a film.

Power and politics in *The Cherry Orchard*

✦ *Activities*

1 Discuss in groups:
a Which characters in the play have power?
b What is the nature of that power?
c How did they acquire that power?

2 Make a diagram or create a pair of tableaux to show the hierarchy of power that exists at the beginning of the play, and at the end of it.

3a Which characters in the play demonstrate any sort of awareness of the changing political situation in Russia?
b Write or improvise a short monologue to summarise what each of them might think about:
  • the coming of the railway to rural Russia
  • the liberation of the serfs
  • the power of the Tsar
  • foreign travel
  • building second homes (*dachas*) on the estate

Characterisation

One of the basic premises of Konstantin Stanislavski's work with actors was to encourage them to understand the 'emotional memory' of the character they were playing. This entailed initially exploring the text of the play to find out as much as possible about the character (what they say, what other people say about them, what their actions reveal about their attitudes, feelings and thought processes), then using the text to create a 'back story' for the character (the character's 'story-so-far'). The purpose of the exercise was to enable the actors to understand why the character behaved in the way they did. Some people have taken the idea too far, developing it into a sort of psychoanalytical exercise, but as long as you keep to what's relevant, it can be very useful.

One of the reasons for exploring a character's 'back story' to this depth is to understand their motivation. Stanislavski realised that being able to identify what a character *wants* at any given moment enables the actor to play a scene far more convincingly. If, for example, you know that what Yasha *wants* at the beginning of Act 2 is to seduce Dunyasha, it makes it very much easier to develop appropriate action around the lines that Chekhov gives you. Yasha is rude to Yepichodov, but not to Charlotta; possibly because he doesn't want Charlotta telling Lyubov that he is insolent. It's unusual for a character to want only one thing, and for that to remain the same throughout the scene. Stanislavski used the term *Objectives* to describe these different wants. Yasha's *overall* Objective is (perhaps) to go back to France with Lyubov, but his immediate Objective is to seduce Dunyasha. This explains why he is not rude to Charlotta and why he sends Dunyasha back to the house as soon as he hears Lyubov and the others. Stanislavski's method not only makes the process of developing a character much more systematic than it had previously been, it also opens up the text, in this instance exposing Yasha's hypocrisy.

◆ *Activities:*

1 Using information you are given in the play, imagine you are one of the following characters, and write your diary entry about any of the incidents that take place *before* the play

starts, and which the character perceives as important (for example, Lopakhin hit by his father and comforted by Lyubov – mentioned on page 15):

- Lyubov Andreyevna Ranyevskaya
- Charlotta
- Lopakhin
- Anya

2 Choose *one* of the following characters, and make a time line on which you mark *all* the events, however trivial, involving this character, which are referred to (directly or indirectly) in the play, but which do *not* happen on stage. Then develop this time line into a brief life history, noting the gaps:

- Lopakhin
- Lyubov
- Firs

3 Working in pairs, look closely at the following scenes. In each instance identify the characters' different objectives, that is, the overriding objective, and the immediate objective at the start of the scene. Note how the immediate objective changes during the scene, and then prepare *one* of the following for presentation to an audience. When you present the scene, ask the audience to identify the objectives they thought you were playing, and to comment on how these objectives change during the scene.

a Act 1, page 24 ('I wish I had good news for you') to page 27 ('Time to go'). Do the exercise for:

- Lopakhin
- Lyubov
- Gayev
- Pishchik

b Act 2, page 48 ('A man appears') to page 49 ('They go, except ANYA and TROFIMOV). Do the exercise for:

- The Man
- Anya
- Varya
- Lyubov
- Gayev
- Lopakhin

c Act 3, page 57 ('You mustn't tease her, Petya') to page 60 ('Petya, wait! I was only joking ...'). Do the exercise for:
- Trofimov
- Lyubov

d Act 4, page 70 ('TROFIMOV enters from outside') to page 73 ('Shut up, they're coming.'). Do the exercise for:
- Trofimov
- Lopakhin
- Anya
- Yasha
- Yepichodov

4 Stanislavski's methods are very productive, but working 'from the inside out' is not the only effective approach to characterisation. It makes sense to explore Lyubov, Lopakhin, Trofimov, Anya and Varya in this way; but Charlotta, Yepichodov, Pishchik and (to a lesser extent) Gayev have their roots in vaudeville and farce. It may be more appropriate to approach them through external appearances. Focusing on Pishchik, Yepichodov and Gayev, do one or more of the following:

a Identify any recognisable 'tics' of behaviour that they are given by Chekhov – their physical characteristics and speech mannerisms.

b Create a still image of each of these characters, as if frozen in the middle of a characteristic gesture. Bring the image to life, exaggerating the gesture, movement or speech mannerism. Then place the character back into one of the scenes in which they are significant. Find ways of using and developing these mannerisms in the context of the play.

c Look through magazines and collections of photographs and try to find photographs of people who look 'right' for these characters.

d Think about the various actors you've seen on TV, film or stage. Who would you cast in these roles?

Triangular relationships

Consider the relationships between characters in the play in which one character is attracted by another, who does not return their love because they desire someone else. Perhaps the most obvious of these is between Yepichodov (the estate clerk), Dunyasha (the maid), and Yasha (the young footman): Yepichodov is 'mad with love' for Dunyasha, who in turn is obsessed by Yasha. There are several other relationships which can be seen as 'triangular'.

✦ *Activity*

Make a note of these triangular relationships, and then:

a Represent these relationships in physical form by creating a still image, which shows how the attractions work, and who has power over whom.

b Go back to the play text, identify, and act out, short extracts (no more than two pages) which show these triangular relationships in action. Aim to make the enactments as physically clear as possible.

Look at the extract (on page 118) from a piece by David Mamet, an American playwright, who has developed a controversial and provocative interpretation of the play from his observations about these triangular relationships.

✦

Who reads / watches *The Cherry Orchard*? How do they interpret it?

The first production of *The Cherry Orchard* in 1904 was popular with Moscow audiences from its first night. It remained in the repertoire of the Moscow Art Theatre until Russia entered the First World War in 1916, when the theatre closed temporarily. Up until that time, the audience for the play would have been predominantly the middle and upper classes of Russian society.

In the immediate aftermath of the Russian Revolution (1918), the play was seen in the Soviet Union as being a nostalgic celebration of a way of life that the Bolshevik ruling party wanted people to forget. *The Cherry Orchard* went out of fashion in Russia, although by 1929 it had been revived by the Moscow Art Theatre, which toured it throughout Europe and America. Over the past fifty years the play has grown in popularity, and it is regularly performed throughout the world – in many different languages. Many of these productions have been very different from the first Moscow Art Theatre production directed by Stanislavski. It is a play that is open to a wide range of interpretations.

Consider how the playing of certain characters might affect people's interpretation of the play.

✦ *Activities*

1 Choose one the following scenes and play it out in such a way that it would be quite clear to an audience which character they were supposed to sympathise with. For the purposes of this exercise, you can play the scene in exaggerated style or naturalistically. Then play it again, trying to get the audience to sympathise with the other character in the scene.

- Lopakhin / Lyubov: Acts 1 and 2 (pp. 24–26 and 40–42) – Lopakhin tries to persuade Lyubov that they have to sell the orchard.
- Trofimov / Anya: Act 2 (pp. 49–51) – Trofimov tells Anya why she and her family have to change.
- Varya / Lopakhin: Act 4 (pp. 76–77) – the near proposal.

2 Now use the work you've done on these scenes to inform the following discussions about the play as a whole:

a Should an audience be encouraged to sympathise with specific characters – and if so, which ones?

b If the audience sympathises with Lyubov, does this necessarily lead to an interpretation of the play as a nostalgic celebration of the 'old order'?

c Who should the audience find more attractive – Lopakhin or Trofimov?

d Some productions of *The Cherry Orchard* have presented Lopakhin very sympathetically, others have suggested that he's clumsy and tactless. How would you present Lopakhin and Trofimov?

'A political and prophetic play'

The Cherry Orchard was first produced in 1904, when Russia was still ruled by Tsar Nicholas II. In 1916, Russia was drawn into the First World War; in 1917 there was a revolution in which the Tsar was ousted from absolute power; and in 1918 a second 'Bolshevik' revolution led to the establishment of a Soviet, communist government and the deaths of the Tsar and all the Russian royal family. One of the intentions of the revolution was to create a society in which wealth was shared between people more equally, and one of the consequences of the revolution was that many wealthy families had their land confiscated: estates like the one owned by Madame Ranyevskaya became the property of the state rather than of individual families.

Consider the following assertions about the play. Each of them comments in some way on the idea that *The Cherry Orchard* is about revolutionary change.

> Virtually everyone wants change; virtually no-one believes it is possible. It is the sensibility of a generation which sits up all night talking about the need for revolution, and is then too tired the next morning to do anything at all, even about its own immediate problems…. Inevitably, such [people] … can seem comic.
>
> (Raymond Williams, *From Ibsen to Brecht*, Chatto and Windus, 1968)

> *The Cherry Orchard* has always seemed to me to be dealing not only with the subjective pain of property loss but also, and more importantly, with its objective necessity.
>
> (Trevor Griffiths, Introduction to his version of *The Cherry Orchard*, Pluto Press, 1978)

> There was no soil for a revolutionary upsurge amid the stifling stagnancy in the air at that time…. Only here and there, underground, were people preparing and gathering strength for the mighty blows. The work of the most progressive people was simply to prepare the mood of society, to implant new ideas and explain the deficiencies of the old life. And Chekhov … was able (like few others) to portray the intolerable atmosphere of stagnation, and to ridicule the vulgarity of the life which it produced…. He was one of the first to sense the inevitability of revolution…. He was one of the first to sound the alarm. Who, if not he, began to cut down the glorious, flowering cherry orchard, realising that it had had its day and that the old life was irrevocably condemned to demolition.
>
> (Konstantin Stanislavski, *Anton Chekhov and the Moscow Art Theatre*, Progress Publishers, Moscow, 1973)

✦ *Activities*

1 Identify those specific moments in *The Cherry Orchard* which demonstrate that Chekhov was at least aware of the possibility of enormous social upheavals in Russia.

2 Divide the class into two groups. One group should argue
the case that *The Cherry Orchard* is a political play, the other
that it is not. Use extracts from the text of the play to support
your argument; and read them aloud to back up your
interpretation.

'A play about sex'

David Mamet, the contemporary American playwright, wrote:

> [*The Cherry Orchard*] is a series of scenes about sexuality, and,
> particularly frustrated sexuality.... The play works because it is
> a compilation of brilliant scenes ... [but] the title is a flag of
> convenience. Nobody in the play gives a damn about the cherry
> orchard.... Why do we cherish the play? Because it is a struggle
> between the Old Values of the Russian aristocracy and their
> loosening grasp on power? I think not. For, finally, a play is
> about – and is *only* about – the actions of its characters. We, as
> audience, understand a play not in terms of ... the social *states*
> of its characters, but only in terms of the *action* the characters
> are trying to accomplish.... The enduring draw of *The Cherry
> Orchard* is not that it's set in a dying Tsarist Russia or that it
> has rich folks and poor folks. We are drawn to the play because
> it speaks to our *subconscious* – which is what a play should do.
> And we subconsciously perceive and enjoy the reiterated action
> of this reiterated scene: two people at odds – each trying to
> fulfil his or her frustrated sexuality.
>
> (David Mamet, 'Notes on *The Cherry Orchard*', from
> *Writing in Restaurants*, Faber & Faber, 1988)

✦ *Activities*

1 Discuss David Mamet's assertions. Even if you do not agree
with everything he is saying, is there any truth in it?

2 He refers to a 'reiterated scene' of 'two people at odds – each
trying to fulfil his or her frustrated sexuality'. This is
certainly one way of describing the relationship between
Dunyasha, Yasha and Yepichodov, but which other
relationships could be described in this way?

3 Which characters in the play are definitely *not* involved in a sexual relationship of some kind? Do they have anything else in common?

4 If it's true that 'nobody ... gives a damn about the cherry orchard', what then (might David Mamet suggest) could Lyubov's 'real' motivation be for returning to the estate?

5 Similarly, given that Lopakhin has become a rich man, why is he so keen to acquire the estate?

6 Whether you find David Mamet's reading of the play appealing or limiting, identify those aspects of the play that it ignores.

The breaking string

The two moments when the stage directions refer to a 'breaking string' (Act 2, top of page 48 and at the very end of the play) are a key to developing an interpretation of the play. The sound comes from outside the action, and whilst it's not specific in a naturalistic sense, it is portentous, an ominous symbol of events beyond the understanding and beyond the control of the characters on stage. When producing the play it can be made to sound naturalistic – like 'a cable in a mine shaft', for example (as Lopakhin himself suggests) – in which case the audience would see Lopakhin as a realist and the others as fantasists. But Chekhov specifically does *not* state that it's the sound of a cable breaking in a mine shaft. He asks for a sound which can *not* be explained easily, a sound which affects the characters and allows their responses to reveal their characters.

✦ *Activities*

1 Experiment with making sounds which might be used here, using both electronic and natural resources.

2 Act out the section from Act 2 from the moment when Yepichodov crosses playing his guitar (p. 47) to Anya's line

'Nothing, Mama. Nothing' (p. 48). Play the extract slowly, paying close attention to the atmosphere that Chekhov wants to create before the string breaks. Use your own sound effect, and explore the effect it has on the characters, paying close attention to the way people respond both in the spoken dialogue and in their physical actions and facial expressions.

◆

GLOSSARY

Act 1

15   **The old nursery:** This is the room which had been a 'nursery' for Lyubov and Gayev when they were children. In other translations of the play the stage direction here reads, 'The room which is still called the nursery'. It is called the 'old nursery', but there have been no children for a long time. It's certainly not Anya's room. She has her own room. (See notes on set design on pages 100 to 105.)

17   **One Foot in the Cowpat:** Dunyasha's nickname for Yepichodov. (See notes on translation on pages 105 to 109.)

19   **Menton:** at that time, a small riviera town, very close to Monte Carlo in Monaco
     kopek: a Russian coin. There are one hundred kopeks in a rouble.

20   **rouble:** a Russian coin. Until the collapse of the Soviet Union, the rouble had for a long time maintained close parity with the pound sterling.

21   **Kiev:** capital of the Ukraine, which was at that time part of the Russian empire

22   **billiards:** A game similar to snooker and pool, but (given Gayev's subsequent references to the game) this is either an obscure Russian version of billiards or Gayev is confused about the rules.
     patchouli: a strong, cheap scent

23   **Kharkov:** an important Ukrainian city, about 650 kilometres (400 miles) south of Moscow

24   **twenty versts:** a verst is a Russian measure of length, about two-thirds of a mile, or just over a kilometre. Twenty versts is about 22 kilometres, just under 15 miles.
     dachas: second homes, or homes in the country

28   **lorgnette:** a pair of spectacles which is held to the eyes on a long handle

31   **the perpetual student:** (See notes for Act 2, page 45.)

32 **Yaroslavl:** an old Russian town on the Volga river, about 250 kilometres (150 miles) north-east of Moscow

Act 2

38 **kvass:** an alcoholic drink, similar to rye beer

39 **Buckle:** H. C. Buckle, an English historian who lived from 1821 to 1862

Avdotya Fyodorovna: a very formal way of addressing Dunyasha – which in itself further reveals Yepichodov's social unease

43 **'So long as you pay, The Germans will play,
And turn our Ivan, To a Frenchie Jean'**

Presumably Lopakhin is gently mocking Lyubov – both for her belief that money can buy almost anything, and also for her internationalism. (See also notes on translation on pages 105 to 109.)

44 **the freedom:** Russian peasants had been officially emancipated in 1861.

45 **The wandering student:** This is a good example of the difficulties that translation can cause. In Britain people who choose to stay on indefinitely at college or university, taking one course after another, are sometimes accused of avoiding the 'real world', of deliberately attempting to postpone getting a job. In Russian, however, the phrase *vyechniy student* means something quite different. Chekhov himself wrote (in a letter to his wife), 'The point is that Trofimov is perpetually being exiled, perpetually being thrown out of university'. So, although Lopakhin (in Act 2) and Varya (in Act 3) are mocking him, Trofimov has effectively been forced to become a perpetual, wandering student because his political convictions are considered dangerous.

46 **Pyotr:** Although Varya calls Trofimov by his first name, it is considerably more formal than calling him Petya, which is the way that Anya and Lyubov address him.

48   **samovar:** a Russian tea urn, in which the tea is kept heated
      by charcoal

49   **'Get thee to a monastery, Ohmelia ...**
      O Nymph in thy prayers remember me!'
      These are misquotations from *Hamlet*. Do you think that
      Lopakhin is deliberately calling her Ohmelia (rather than
      Ophelia, the character in *Hamlet*)? In the Russian the
      distorted misquotations incorporate the Russian words for
      hops and intoxication. The various different translations
      include one which reads, 'Ophelia – hop along and get thee
      to a nunnery. ... Nymph, in thy prisons be all my sins – and
      double gins – remembered.'

Act 3

53   **Caligula's horse:** Caligula was a Roman Emperor who
      promoted his horse to become a Senator.

54   **Caucasian:** from the Caucasus, a mountainous region to the
      south of Russia

55   **'Guter Mensch aber schlechter Musikant':** a German saying.
      In Russian, Chekhov did not supply the subsequent free
      translation. What does this tell you about the audience for
      the play?

56   **The perpetual student:** (See notes above for Act 2, page 45.)

60   **Alexis Tolstoy:** Alexis Tolstoy was a sentimental and much
      derided poet – not to be confused with Leo Tolstoy, the
      author of *Anna Karenina* and *War and Peace*.

Act 4

76   **Varvara Mihailovna:** the formal way of addressing Varya

77   **seventy versts:** about 75 kilometres, just under 50 miles

FURTHER READING

Anton Chekhov

The four full length plays
The Seagull (1896)

Uncle Vanya (1899)

Three Sisters (1901)

The Cherry Orchard (1904)

Pam Gems (the translator of this edition) has also translated *Uncle Vanya* (1992) and *The Seagull* (1994). Both plays are published by Nick Hern Books.

Vaudevilles
The best known are:

Swan Song (1888)

The Bear (1888)

The Proposal (1890)

All the above are available in a single collection, translated by Michael Frayn (*Plays by Anton Chekhov*, Methuen, 1991).

Short stories
The Duel and other stories (translated by Ronald Wilks, Penguin Classics, 1984)

Lady with Lapdog and other stories (translated by David Magarshack, Penguin Classics, 1964)

Of the many available editions of Chekhov's short stories, these two contain some of the most accessible and enjoyable stories.

Other

Selected Letters of Anton Chekhov (Lillian Hellman (ed.), Picador, 1984)

Plays by other Russian playwrights:

Nikolai Gogol, *The Government Inspector* (1836)

An extremely funny play, which seems remarkably up to date.

Mikhail Bulgakov, *The White Guard* (1926; available in translation in a Methuen edition)

A play set during the Civil War that followed the Russian revolutions of 1917. The play is in some ways quite Chekhovian in that it offers a large cast and complex characterisation – with characters struggling to come to terms with the massive changes occurring around them. Bulgakov shares with Chekhov an ability to write humorously about very serious situations.

Novels

Mikhail Bulgakov, *Black Snow* (translated by Michael Glenny, Collins Harvill, 1967)

A richly comic autobiographical novel about getting a play staged, in which the Moscow Art Theatre is thinly disguised as the 'Independent Theatre' and Stanislavski as Ivan Vasilievich.

Leo Tolstoy, *Anna Karenina* (Penguin Classics, 1954; first published 1874–1876)

Ivan Turgenev, *Sketches from a Hunter's Album* (translated by Richard Freeborn, Penguin Classics, 1990; first published 1852)

Stories about Russian provincial life and the tyranny of serfdom.

Commentary

Edward Braun, *The Director and the Stage* (Methuen, 1982)

This includes excellent chapters on the development of naturalism and on the relationship between Stanislavski and Chekhov.

David Mamet, *Writing in Restaurants* (Faber & Faber, 1988)

J. L. Styan, *Chekhov in Performance* (Cambridge University Press, 1971)

Russian history

Hans Rogger (ed.), *Russia in the Age of Modernisation and Revolution* (Longman, 1992)

Miscellaneous

Banham, M. (ed.), *The Cambridge Guide to Theatre* (Cambridge University Press, 1995)

Stanislavski, K., *An Actor Prepares* (translated by Elizabeth R. Hapgood, Routledge, 1967; first published 1936)

CAMBRIDGE LITERATURE

◆

Ben Jonson *The Alchemist*

William Wycherley *The Country Wife*

William Blake *Selected Works*

Jane Austen *Pride and Prejudice*

Mary Shelley *Frankenstein*

Charlotte Brontë *Jane Eyre*

Emily Brontë *Wuthering Heights*

Nathaniel Hawthorne *The Scarlet Letter*

Charles Dickens *Hard Times*

Charles Dickens *Great Expectations*

George Eliot *Silas Marner*

Thomas Hardy *Far from the Madding Crowd*

Henrik Ibsen *A Doll's House*

Robert Louis Stevenson *Treasure Island*

Mark Twain *Huckleberry Finn*

Thomas Hardy *Tess of the d'Urbervilles*

Kate Chopin *The Awakening and other stories*

Anton Chekhov *The Cherry Orchard*

James Joyce *Dubliners*

Six Poets of the Great War

D. H. Lawrence *Selected Short Stories*

Edith Wharton *The Age of Innocence*

F. Scott Fitzgerald *The Great Gatsby*

Virginia Woolf *A Room of One's Own*

Robert Cormier *After the First Death*

Caryl Churchill *The After-Dinner Joke*
and *Three More Sleepless Nights*

Graham Swift *Learning to Swim*

Fay Weldon *Letters to Alice*

Louise Lawrence *Children of the Dust*

Julian Barnes *A History of the World in 10½ Chapters*

Amy Tan *The Joy Luck Club*

Four Women Poets

Moments of madness – one hundred years of short stories

Helen Edmundson *The Mill on the Floss*